Leonardo da Vinci: Biography, Art Work and Inventions

by

Tom Brown

COPYRIGHT

Copyright © 2016 by Rainbow Press

All rights reserved. No part of this publication may be reproduced, distributed, or transmitted in any form or by any means, including photocopying, recording, or other electronic or mechanical methods, without the prior written permission of the publisher, except in the case of brief quotations embodied in critical reviews and certain other noncommercial uses permitted by copyright law.

Rainbow Press

Table of Contents

Leonardo da Vinci: Biography, Art Work and Inventions 1
by 1
Tom Brown 1
COPYRIGHT 2
Table of Contents 3
Childhood (1452-1467) 11
Apprenticeship (1467-1476) 15
Troubles (1476-1482) 22
Moving to Milan (1482-1489) 27
The Last Supper (1490-1499) 32
Military Engineering (1500-1503) 39
Return to Home and The Mona Lisa 44
Back to Milan (1506-1513) 49
Life in Rome (1513-1516) 52
France (1516-1519) 57
PERSONAL RELATIONS 60
Salai 60
Verrocchio 71
Machiavelli 73
Michelangelo 75
Melzi 81
INVENTIONS 83
Anemometer 83
Flying Machine 85
Parachute 90
33-Barreled Organ 92
Tank-Armored Car 94
Giant Crossbow 96
Triple Barrel Canon 98
Clock 100
Colossus 102
Ideal City 104
Robotic Knight 106
Self-Propelled Cart 108
Scuba Gear 110
Revolving Bridge 112

The Ball Bearing 114
Cluster Bomb 116
Scythed Chariots 118
Fortress 120
ART WORK 122
Annunciation 122
The Baptism of Christ...125
Madonna of the Carnation 129
Ginevra de' Benci..132
Benois Madonna 136
The Adoration of the Magi...141
St. Jerome in the Wilderness..146
Madonna Litta...149
Virgin of the Rocks...152
Portrait of a Musician 164
Lady with an Ermine 168
La belle ferronnière 173
Sala delle Asse 176
The Virgin and Child with St Anne and St John the Baptist...........179
Portrait of Isabella d'Este..185
The Madonna of the Yarnwinder..189
Bacchus..194
Salvator Mundi 197
Self-portrait of Leonardo da Vinci 202
The Battle of Anghiari 205
Leda and the Swan..212
St. John the Baptist 216
Vitruvian Man...220
The Last Supper..226
Mona Lisa 233
SECRETS AND THEORIES 243
Speculations about Mona Lisa...243
Columns and Trimming:..243
Copies 244
Nude versions 245
Infrared scan 246
Eyebrows and eyelashes 247
Subject 248
Pregnancy 250

The 251
Golden triangle, rectangle and spiral 251
The Last Supper 253
Food 253
Mary Magdalene 254
Mirrored Version 254
The Knife 254
The Music 255
ENDING 255
Other Works Recommended For You 257

Leonardo di ser Piero da Vinci, was an Italian genius, inventor and painter whose areas of interest included architecture, science, music, mathematics, engineering, literature, anatomy, geology, astronomy, botany, writing, history, invention, painting, sculpting and cartography.

As we all know, he is considered one of the greatest painters of all time. He has been called the father of paleontology, ichnology and architecture. Some of his most famous inventions, parachute, helicopter and tank are still in important use in our day.

Many historians describe Leonardo as the "Universal Genius" and "Renaissance Man". They claim he had an "unquenchable curiosity" and "feverishly inventive imagination."

His mind and personality are on extraordinary limits, he himself is mysterious and remote.

What a great opportunity we have, we can study this legend's life and works together!

Childhood (1452-1467)

In the Tuscan hill town of Vinci, a boy named Leonardo was born on 15 April 1452. Little did they know, this boy had great talent in him and would soon influence the whole world for the centuries to come.

This boy was a out of wedlock son of a wealthy man named Messer Piero Fruosino di Antonio da Vinci and a peasant named Caterina. The man was a Florentine legal notary, da Vinci meaning "of Vinci".

Thus, the boy took the name of "Lionardo di ser Piero da Vinci" meaning "Leonardo, (son) of (Mes)ser Piero from Vinci". The "ser" in the title meant that he was the son of a gentleman. Leonardo's father took him into his own custody when he was three years old.

There is not much we know about Leonardo's childhood. But we certainly know that he at least recorded some of his earliest childhood memory in his notebooks. While explaining his obsession with devising a machine for flying, he explains that as a baby, a kite landed on him and stuck its tail feathers into his mouth, repeatedly hitting his lips with its feathers. We don't know if someone told him about that or he was old enough to remember it, one thing was certain. This experience was certainly traumatic, and historians believe that it would indeed have influenced the boy to gain interest in flight.

   He spent his first three years in Anchiano, in the home of his mother. Then his father took him into his own custody, thus he started living in Francesco, a small town of Vinci.

   At any rate, Leonardo probably spent most of his time as a child with neither parent, but with his paternal uncle Francesco, who would later remember Leonardo in his will. Ser Piero was busy in the nearby city of Florence, and Caterina had married a man named Accattabriga. Francesco worked as a farmer, and Leonardo probably spent a great deal of his childhood out of doors, observing nature and possibly sketching it.

   Leonardo's status as an illegitimate child certainly affected his personal development. Although the upper classes of the quatrocento usually ignored illegitimacy, allowing bastard sons to inherit their fathers' property and power, the middle classes were quite particular. As a notary, Leonardo's father Ser Piero was positioned quite solidly within the developing middle classes, which were full of clubs, guilds, and unions that carefully regulated the opportunities of a boy like Leonardo.

As a bastard, he would never be able to attend a university or even become a notary like his father. Also, Leonardo no doubt felt neglected by his parents. Not only was he illegitimate, but his mother was soon distracted by her legitimate children, and Ser Piero probably spent most of his time away from Leonardo, in Florence.

Thus lacking anyone in whose footsteps he was expected to follow, Leonardo could develop freely into the universal man he would become. He spent his days with his uncle Francesco, tending to animals and exploring farmland, observing the nature and landscapes that he would later sketch and study. Because he was not expected to become a notary, he was free to pursue drawing. Also, although as a notary Ser Perio probably ensured that the boy had a proper "elementary" education, Leonardo had to learn many things for himself, thus initiating what would become his habitual auto didacticism; he would later teach himself Latin, physics, and human anatomy.

Even as a child, Leonardo showed his talents strongly. One time, a local peasant made himself a round shield and requested that Ser Piero have it painted for him. Ser

Piero let Leonardo paint the shield. Leaonardo drew a painting of a monster spitting fire which was so terrifying and magnificent at the same time, Ser Piero sold it to a Florentine art dealer. Then the Duke of Milan bought the same piece from that art dealer. Following that, Ser Piero bought a shield decorated with a heart pierced by an arrow and gave it to the peasant, making a profit at the same time.

Apprenticeship (1467-1476)

Unlike most children on his age, Leonardo was a devoted artist. Ser Piero recognized his talents, especially when he painted the shield a peasant gave him. This is why Ser Piero apprenticed him to a studio.

Since Leonardo was an illegitimate child, this opportunity was the best thing he could hope for. Ser Piero's many clients belonged to the priesthood anyway, he probably had a good heart of the art market. He took his boy to one of the most respected workshops in the city which belonged to one and only: Andrea del Verrocchio.

Donatello himself taught artistry to Verrocchio. Verrocchio also served as official sculptor to the ruling Medici family. He was always better and more passionate about sculpting than painting.

Verrocchio was not only a skilled artist. He was an exceptional teacher too. Leonardo received training in all artistic genres, except for large wall murals and frescoes.

He was only 15 years old when he first went to study under Verrocchio in 1467, a mere boy. He needed to perform simple chores at first, as apprenticeship required.

He was like a servant almost. One by one, he learned to prepare pigments and canvases, then he drew the studies of Verrocchio's works and other models.

Florence was in a golden era as a city when Leonardo was growing up. That can only mean Leonardo spent a good time in society, especially given that the ruler of Florence, Lorenzo de Medici, liked to hold public festivals as frequently as possible. There is no doubt Leonardo attended these, happily enjoying the riches and emotions.

Leonardo's earliest known drawing, Arno Valley, dates from a feast day. It is a landscape painting, probably the result of him wandering the countryside while the city was in noisy festival. The attention to geologic and botanic detail in the drawing stands out the most.

During the Renaissance, it was customary to draw paintings by groups of artists, directed by a master. It was in Verrocchio's Baptism of Christ Leonardo's first known contribution lies. Almost all experts agree that Leonardo painted the leftmost angel. Its face and hair have a graceful quality unlike the other figures in the painting. It is also guessed that Leonardo was responsible for the background.

Vasari, Leonardo's first biographer, states that Verrocchio was so impressed with his pupil's work on the angel that he became ashamed of his own talents and swore never to paint again.

Verrocchio: The Baptism of Christ

Indeed, Verrocchio dropped painting soon, but the more likely explanation is he simply decided that Leonardo was good enough to take over most of the workshop's painting so Verrocchio could focus on his sculpture works. He always preferred sculptures anyway. And he was excellent at them. Sooner than later, Leonardo started doing works of his own, including the Annunciation.

The Annunciation

Some experts hold the idea of that Leonardo was responsible for the background vista in the Annunciation and no more. Some experts suggest that he also painted the painting's angel. The sleeve of the angel matches some sketches from one of Leonardo's notebooks too.

The wings are strangely realistic that can easily attributed to Leonardo, especially when we think of his interest in birds. Not all the experts think the same unfortunately. Some say that the head of the angel is too flat to be the work of Leonardo.

It is unknown for a certainty if Leonardo was involved in the painting's actual execution. But it is highly possible that he sketched the composition and let others do the painting. By only one look at the painting, I am sure you can appreciate the beauty of it. And the genius behind.

He was very lucky to have a master who was renowned throughout the Florence and had the greatest patrons of the Renaissance, Medici family. This contributed greatly to Leonardo, giving his career a strong start.

Leonardo acquired a tendency to paint curly bunched hair to create triangular compositions and to paint girlish, stylized faces from his master, Verrocchio. As expected, many of these habits wore off and Leonardo's own style matured, as he matured himself. And of course, even while he was an apprentice, his own style showed through.

Experts did an x-ray of Verrocchio's Baptism. It revealed that Leonardo's brushstrokes are much lighter than those of his master, and it is obvious to the naked eye that he was the greater talent.

The difference of talent didn't cause any envy or conflict between the methodical master Verrocchio and his genius pupil, da Vinci.

Leonardo built a reputation to himself as his inability to finish many of his projects. Despite this, he seems to have been capable of great discipline, as it is shown by his ability to teach himself Latin and Anatomy. He used cadavers for that. One can only hope to have as great a pupil as him.

Leonardo spent first few years of his life in countryside. Growing up, he must have been in awe of the city of Florence. His artistic talents thrived any of his counterparts, but he was not as sophisticated. Perhaps his love of luxury and fine clothes later in life stemmed from the envy he felt as a Florentine youth of small means.

Troubles (1476-1482)

It was 1476. Everything was going well for Leonardo. He was becoming a master on his own right. Almost like a partner to Verrocchio. Until things started to turn bad. Leonardo suddenly got infected with a scandal.

He was accused of sodomy along with three other young men. Who accused them is still a mystery to this day. Sodomy was a criminal offense in Renaissance Florence at that time. However in most cases, authorities chose to look other way and the general culture attached little social stigma to homosexuality.

He was only 24 years old at the time. They specifically accused him with a homosexuality interaction with a notorious prostitute, Jacopo Saltarelli.

Lucky for him, the charges were dismissed three months after, due to a lack of witnesses and evidence. It is highly likely that the Medici family had something to do with the result of the case. Because there was a Medici family member among the defendants, Lionardo de Tornabuoni. Lorenzo de Medici's mother had been a Tornabuoni.

Immediately following the case, Leonardo spend his time very productively. In the mid 1470s, he worked on the Portrait of Ginevra da Benci. He also received his first commission around 1478, a religious group demanded him to paint an Adoration of the Shepherds.

"I have begun the two Virgin Marys." Leonardo wrote in his journals in 1478. Experts agree that the Benois Madonna is one of them. It was originally believed lost. But when a travelling musician sold it to a Russian in southern Italy in the nineteenth century, it shocked everyone. In 1909, experts confirmed that it was indeed a work of Leonardo da Vinci.

Benois Madonna

In the painting, the Christ Child plays with two small flowers on Mary's lap in a serious manner. Both have halos. The Virgin also has a glowing, rounded face which points out that it was one of Leonardo's earlier work. she looks appealing and fresh, unlike the blandness of other artists' madonnas from the time.

When he got 30 years old, he was working pretty much independently from Verrocchio. He received a commission for The Adoration of the Magi but he soon left Florence for Milan, so it remains unfinished. Even though it is unfinished, critics still think that it is a masterpiece.

The painting shows Leonardo's ability to bestow a familiar scene with a different and lively spirit. Leonardo once said: "A good painter has two subjects of primary importance: man and the state of man's mind. The first is easy, the second difficult, since it must be conveyed by means of the gestures and movements of the various parts of the body."

Usually in religious paintings, figures stood placidly as if they were separated from the scene's focal point by a gap of centuries. However Leonardo is very keen on realism. That explains why the result is more entertaining.

Another painting he left unfinished before his departure to Milan is Saint Jerome.

Leonardo's leaving the Florence doesn't come as a surprise even though he was pretty successful in there. He wasn't able to complete two major commissions he received. Two "Adorations." On top of that, he was charged with sodomy. Even though the case was dismissed, it was more important than it looks in Leonardo's life.

It might be the start of a lifetime of paranoia on Leonardo's part. He frequently chose to drew absurd pictures of gossiping townspeople and he declared malicious gossip as a serious evil.

The other important aspect of the incident was the question of Leonardo's sexuality. Homosexuality was common in that time and several things indicate that Leonardo could have been gay. He never married. No recorded evidence could be found regarding him showing interest to a women. He also wrote in his notebooks that male-female intercourse disgusted him. His male anatomical drawings exhibit much more detail to sexual organs than its counterpart. On top of that, Leonardo chose beautiful young males such as Salai and Melzi to assist him with.

Moving to Milan (1482-1489)

Leonardo da Vinci moved to Milan in 1482. Although he was now a master, he wasn't satisfied with his life in Florence for the reasons I have pointed out before. There was another thing that drew his interest as much as painting: science. Other than paintings, he also had begun making copious scientific speculations in his notebooks. Milan was less artistically centered than Florence. Still, he did get more than enough opportunities to apply his various interests.

Leonardo set his eyes on the top. He probably wanted the opportunity to work for Milan's ruler, Ludovico Sforza. Milan held a very important strategic position in southwestern Europe, therefore often a point of military contention. Leonardo wrote a letter to Sforza before coming to the city, stating that he wanted to offer his services as a military engineer.

Whether or not Leonardo sent the letter, it certainly proves that Leonardo had really strong interest in military engineering. In the meantime, da Vinci designed a few military machines, including a basic form of war tank and a wild chariot with scythes attached to its wheels.

Leonardo also planned a gigantic horse to serve as a monument for Sforza. Sforza always hoped to erect a magnificent monument like this in honor of his father. This horse would require a good level of engineering as well as art. And he also mentioned this gigantic horse in his letter.

However, when Leonardo first arrived in Milan, his first major project was another painting, the famous " Virgin of the Rocks."

Da Vinci painted the work for the Confraternity of the Immaculate Conception in Milan. The side panels painted by two brothers named de Predis. Unfortunately, the contract caused many legal problems, so much so that Leonardo eventually had to supervise the painting of a second version of the painting almost 24 years later, 1506.

Virgin of the Rocks

The Virgin's placement on rocks is the most astonishing aspect about the Virgin of the Rocks. Leonardo liked using hazy, rocky background and this provides the extreme example. The most mature woman we have seen him paint at this point on his career is the Virgin herself. Unlike the stylized faces of his earlier paintings, her head is longer and more natural than the round. The Christ Child rests at her feet while John the Baptist toddles at her right and an angel sits to her left.

While he invested so much time in this complex painting, Leonardo was beginning serious research into anatomy on the side. To be able to learn more things about the workings of the human body, he learned to dissect cadavers. The sketches and diagrams he made about the human body are some of the most accurate studies of the human body made before the twentieth century.

He didn't stop when he fully recorded the known structure and functions of the body, he also made countless revolutionary discoveries about anatomy, all of which contradicted contemporary medical beliefs. The fire burning inside of him about anatomy didn't stop until he was dead. He wanted to collect every founding and sketch of human body into a book called "Of the Human Figure." However, like so many of his paintings, none of these books ever came to completion.

It appears so that Leonardo have become an outstanding figure in Sforza's court fairly soon after his arrival in Milan. He worked on two famous portraits during the 1480s, the "Portrait of a Musician" and the "Lady with an Ermine". He also began working on the bronze horse I have mentioned before.

Sforza wasn't actually the legitimate ruler of Milan, this is why he was too eager to erect monuments that would remind the town of his heritage and authority. The large horseman statue was to honor his father. Not surprisingly, Leonardo planned a horse that would stand twenty feet tall and comprise 200,000 pounds of bronze. No bronze statue ever came close to this size, Leonardo didn't have the chance to cast it too. He still continued to work on different designs, molds and models throughout the 1480s and 1490s. The project wasted a great deal of his time, and was one of his greatest failures. On top of it, when the French invaded Milan in 1499, archers used the model to practice crossbows.

In his time in Milan, he would conduct intense scientific investigations in his spare time, while working on one or two major public projects, doing a few portraits on the side. This pattern of work would consist throughout his life.

The Last Supper (1490-1499)

The year 1490 pointed out the arrival of a new member to the artist's household, ten year old body Giacomo, also known as "Salai." according to da Vinci's journals.

Salai was a beautiful boy from a peasant family. The precise nature of his relationship with Leonardo isn't clear, however the master seemed quite fondly towards him. Leonardo showered him with gifts and never punished him for his constant thievery. They lived together until they got separated by the cold claws of dead. However, they would constantly argue with each other, and for some reason, it appears that he received less at Leonardo's death than what seemed appropriate.

It is highly suspected that "Caterina" his mother came to live with Leonardo in 1493. Some historians also agree that she may be a servant. However, some of the few vague personal notes in Leonardo's notebooks suggest that he had invited her, as opposed to hiring her. Also the woman who came in 1493 died a few years later, suitable for his mother's age.

It was also traditionally appropriate for mothers to come and live with their children after their husbands' deaths in Leonardo's day. However Leonardo's accounts show that he spent suspiciously little on her funeral. Maybe he wanted to avoid a noticeable funeral, not wanting to draw attention to his illegitimacy and dishonor his mother.

Leonardo began working on a large wall painting for Sforza in 1495. Sforza ate dinner in the refectory of the convent of Santa Maria delle Grazie twice a week. He wanted a large portrayal of Jesus' Last Supper to hang on the wall facing the head table.

We all know that The Last Supper and the Mona Lisa are easily Leonardo's most famous paintings. Millions have seen the reproduction of The Last Supper but only few realize that it is not only a masterful painting, but also an optical illusion. Leonardo painted the painting on the wall of a refectory, he intended it to appear an extension of the room itself. He achieved this effect by the painting's perspective, which matches the lines of the room.

The table of Christ floated above the heads of the dining monks. There were of course other purposes for this specific perspective. Its lines focus on Christ's head, which is cleverly framed by an open window, a kind of circumstantial halo.

The pious would say that Leonardo wanted to show that Jesus' natural grace provided him with this divine framing, that Leonardo abandoned painting gold discs because they were artificial.

The German writer Goethe, argues otherwise. He suggests that Leonardo left out halos as a gesture toward secularizing the myth of Jesus.

No matter what his true purpose was, he took special care to follow scriptural details. The seating arrangements were reflecting Bible's description, however to achieve this Leonardo worked as opposed to traditional quattrocento arrangements. Instead of Judas sitting on the opposite side of the table, he was the third man to Christ's right in The Last Supper, clutching a moneybag.

Christ forms a regal triangle with his body; like the Virgins of Adoration of the Magi or Virgin of the Rocks; his disciples form rippling waves. In the painting, he has just announced that one of them will betray him but he has not yet indicated that it is in fact Judas.

Each disciple in the painting is eager to acquit himself or trying to identify the future traitor. The disciples on the far right recoil in surprise what the group next to them leans toward Christ with curiosity. Divided into groups of three, each group has a slightly different reaction to the news.

Unconventionally, the hands of the disciples contradict the movement of their bodies, while giving the whole composition a flowing circuit that always leads back to the center. Leonardo da Vinci shows his ability to animate a scene that had become clichéd through countless previous depictions, as he did in the Adoration of the Magi.

Leonardo lacked significant knowledge of the correct wall painting technical process, because his master, Verrocchio, had not been an expert in wall painting too. He tried to invent his own paint mixtures, insisting on painting with oils on the wall. This particular style didn't suit wall painting. As a result, the painting began to deteriorate almost immediately.

The famous mathematician Fra Luca Pacioli came to stay in Milan while Leonardo was working on The Last Supper. Since Leonardo was an illegitimate child, he had been denied secondary education. Because of this reason, he couldn't even perform simple algebra. But he had always had an interest in numbers and math, this is why he eagerly learned from Pacioli despite the obstacles. Pacioli must have shared a mutual awe for his student, since Leonardo already designed and discovered so many things, without knowing algebra.

The two collaborated on a book eventually, called De divina proportione. Leonardo drew the illustrations, while decorating the La Sala delle Asse at the same time.

The political situation in Milan took a turn for the worse in 1499. Apparently, the French had begun an invasion of Lombardy, causing Sforza to instantly fleeing to Germany. Eventually, the French conquered the city. Leonardo and his math teacher Pacioli left together for Mantua afterwards.

Sforza tried to recapture Milan using Swiss mercenaries eventually. However a big surprise was waiting for him. His forces took a bribe from the French and betrayed him.

Leonardo was 47 at the time of the invasion. His three greatest paintings at that point were the *Adoration of the Magi,* which was incomplete, the *Virgin of the Rocks,* which was ensnared in a legal battle over rights to its ownership, and the magnificent *Last Supper,* which was already deteriorating.

The drawing of The Last Supper had a bigger purpose. Something that would be permanent, something that would be painted on stone as opposed to canvas, however the mural was nor already vanishing.

Even though people thought of Leonardo as a master, everybody agreed that he seemed incapable of creating anything that would last, eventually.

Not only his paintings were in bad shape, even his model for the giant bronze horse had met its destruction at the hands of the French soldiers, as a practice target. We can only conclude that he was a dissatisfied man.

Despite all of the negatives thing he experienced, there is one thing that cheered him up. The entry of Salai into Leonardo's household. Whatever their relationship, Leonardo held a great fondness for the boy.

After Salai's arrival, he would take a series of young male pupils into his household. If the Caterina who also joined him in his house was actually his mother, he had a lot of things to be happy for now.

It is a terrific thing that even in the face of so many failures, Leonardo still devoured new fields of research. He quickly attached himself to Pacioli, allowing his skills to become more eclectic in the coming years.

Military Engineering (1500-1503)

Leonardo and Pacioli traveled to Mantua as soon as they left Milan. In Mantua, Leonardo worked for a short time on a portrait of the generous if overbearing patron of the arts, Isabelle d'Este. Surprise surprise, he never finished the work, despite frequent and nagging letters from Isabelle over the course of the next five years.

Leonardo proceeded to Venice in 1500. The French invasion of Lombardy and Sforza's failed attempt to mount a counter attack out of exile had embroiled much of the Mediterranean coast in war.

While the Venice was still in a war with the Ottoman Empire, Leonardo went to the Senate of Venice and offered his services as an engineer. He presented his plan to construct a kind of mobile dam that would allow Venetian forces to draw the Turks into the Isonzo river valley and then flood the valley wiping out the enemy forces.

Whether they liked this plan or not, the senate didn't act on his plan. He also came up with a diving apparatus in the hopes of initiating an underwater raid on the Ottoman fleet, drilling holes in the bottoms of their ships.

Surprisingly, his design was remarkably similar to modern scuba gear. the senate didn't act on this plan too. Luckily, Leonardo was able to keep the details of his designs secret, not letting them fall into the wrong hands.

He then returned to Florence by April. He went to his father to see him. Ser Piero was now a wealthy old man of 74, living with his fourth wife. Leonardo took up lodgings with the Servite friars of Florence, hoping to find a patron soon. He agreed to paint an altarpiece for the friars however as usual it took him months to begin.

But he wasn't idle in the mean time. He undertook several architectural projects and continued work in his notebooks about the collapse of buildings and building materials.

At the time, there was much discussion of an apocryphal passage which claimed that St. Anne, Mary's mother, was also a virgin mother. This is why he was hired to paint an altarpiece of the Virgin and Saint Anne for the friars.

He began the preliminary painting by 1501 but the painting itself was never finished, however he didn't forget about it. He worked on it time to time over the years. But perhaps, the painting is even more beautiful incomplete than it would be if Leonardo completed it.

In the painting, the Virgin, sits with her mother St. Anne. Anne's face is dark and mysterious as if she is going to tell the fate of Jesus, while Mary remains warm and content. Mary seems eager to keep the Child with her, although the child seems to be already interested in tending "his flock."

In 1502 Leonardo heard the good news. He finally got the chance to act as a military engineer. Cesare Borgia, who Leonardo might have met with in Milan, was the commander of the pope's army. He had almost conquered all of central Italy, the Romagna.

Borgia took on Leonardo as his chief military engineer. Leonardo traveled the Tuscan coast to inspect fortifications and drain marshes. Afterwards he travelled all over the Romagna, ending up in Imola eventually. This is where Borgia set up his winter quarters. An attack was expected, thus the city was heavily fortified.

Leonardo probably met Niccolo Machiavelli at Imola, before seeing him again in Florence next year. Leonardo probably got along well with Borgia, both were ambitious, illegitimate, unconventional men.

Leonardo da Vinci drew perhaps the first directly overhead map of a city, in addition to his official military duties. Typical maps of that time assumed a vantage from an angle, a bird's eye view.

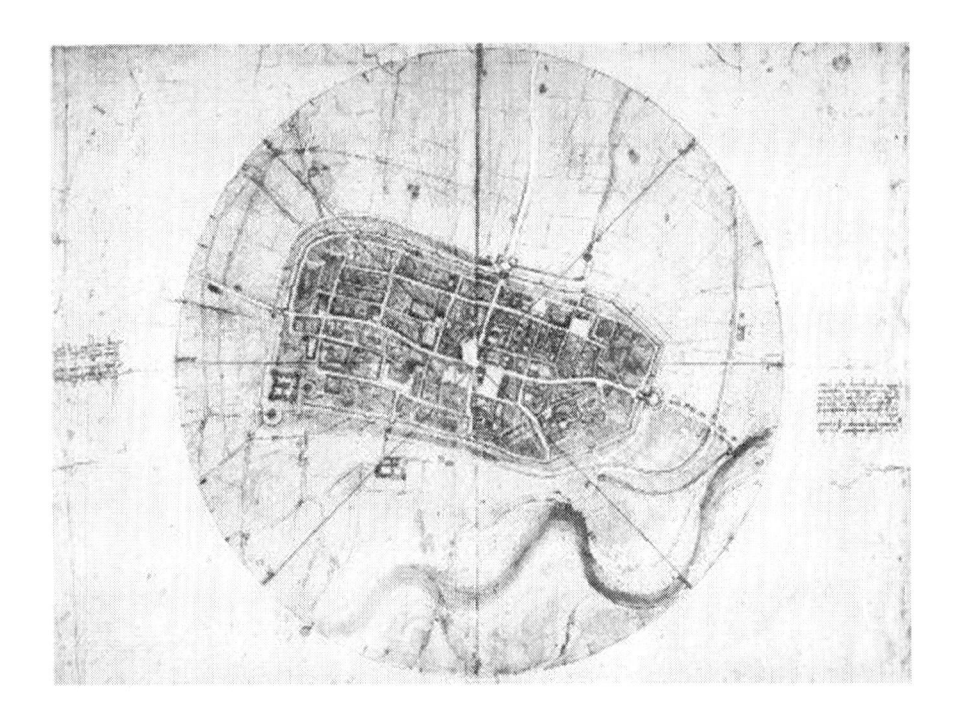

Town of Imola

It is guessed that Leonardo planned to return to Milan at first. It was expected from Sforza that he would regain power, but these hopes were destroyed when Sforza was betrayed by his Swiss mercenaries. Leonardo didn't appear loyal to the duke anyway. The Ottomans were attacking Venice because of Sforza's bidding after all. Sforza wanted to retake Lombardy by distracting Venice, an ally of France.

Leonardo da Vinci was anxious to come up with scientific methods to defeat the Turks and win the war for Venice quickly. He didn't let his designs fall into the hands of the criminal but he didn't seem to care which side of the war used them too. Similarly, Leonardo did not seem to mind working for Cesare Borgia, who was renowned as an incestuous, impious man who had liaisons with his sister, had his brother murdered, and held as much responsibility for the corruption of the church as anyone else. It seems Leonardo's prime loyalty was to science.

Leonardo achieved great fame when he finally returned to Florence as a 48 years old. But he accomplished very few of his goals. People didn't trust him to finish a commission. His city changed big time but his father was still alive.

The religious zealot Fra Savonarola took power in Florence, causing the Medici family to lose the control of the city, however temporarily. Fra Savonarola accused the Church with impiety and ordered the burning of all books he found sinful.

Although Savonarola had been burned at the stake himself by the time Leonardo made his way to Florence, some still appreciated his thoughts. No doubt, this troubled da Vinci.

Return to Home and The Mona Lisa

Leonardo left his post with Cesare Borgia in 1503 for unknown reasons. Maybe he didn't like some of the assassinations Borgia pulled off in recent months, maybe he knew Borgia's power would come to an end soon.

Pisa and Florence were at war back then. The Arno River ran from Florence to Pisa. And as a director of the project, it was Machiavelli himself that divert the river so as to prevent it from running through Pisa, thus depriving the inhabitants of fresh water, as well as supplies brought by riverboats.

This is the reason that experts think Leonardo met with Machiavelli again. It was Leonardo who made many sketches of the river and planned a new course, most likely the directors consulted him as an engineer. However, the project itself failed to do its job.

Leonardo gained a huge reputation by this time, and Florence wanted to take advantage of its famous citizen. He was commissioned by the new, Republican government. The government had built a large council hall at the Pallazzo della Signora. They commissioned

Leonardo to paint the Battle of Anghiari, memorializing a historical Florentine battle on one of the large side walls.

Leonardo had technical problems on his last mural, The Last Supper. The same problems occurred again. And it doomed the painting to failure. As expected, it deteriorated very quickly, and the painter abandoned it in 1505, long before it was completed.

The only records that have been left behind for us to find out are a few of Leonardo's sketches and copies done by other artists like Rubens. It wasn't even the original that belonged the Leonardo, Rubens's style shows through in the copy.

Leonardo knew that wars were beastly things, and he meant the Battle of Anghiari to illustrate its horrors.

Experts agree that Leonardo started his work on the Mona Lisa while he was still in Florence, probably around 1505. The debate around the painting's subject went on for years.

Some people used computer technology to compare the portrait with Leonardo's own self-portrait and suggests that the Mona Lisa is a female version of Leonardo da Vinci. Some people agree on that the subject was actually Leonardo's lover, Salai.

Other arguments assert that the figure is the wife of Francesco del Gioconda. However if this is true, she never received the portrait, since Leonardo took the painting to France with him. The French Royal family took the painting for themselves after Leonardo's death. But then the French Revolution happened. After that, Louvre was opened to the public and the painting became the property of the French people.

Unfortunately the Mona Lisa has been damaged by the layers of dirt and varnish that darkened the painting. However most of the impact sourced from the fame of the painting itself. Still, nothing can beat a closer look with a naked eye.

The head of the woman is round and full of flesh, contrary to the flat head of the Portrait of Ginevra de Benci of 1474.

One can describe Leonardo's painting career as a quest for perfect female head. The Mona Lisa is relatively mute in coloration not only due to fading but due to the artist's intentions.

Leonardo's preference for the shadows and veils and other things possible in oil painting reached its apex in this portrait, where color and light are in perfect contingency to volume. The background is typically what you can expect from Leonardo, rock crags and mists.

Leonardo got called back to Milan at the bidding of the French government briefly. But it is guessed that while still in Florence, he probably made his second attempt to build a flying machine and operate it. His first time was made some time in the late 1490s, in Milan.

He designed bird like gliders and machines that looked like modern day helicopters. Birds always had huge impact on him since his childhood. He based all of his studies on flight and aerodynamics on observations of birds, elegantly sketching the creatures' wing movement.

These years were Leonardo's most productive years in his life. The Battle of Anghiari enjoyed great commendation although it would eventually deteriorate. The second painter was working on what would be the hall's second mural. Who was he? Michelangelo of course. His painting wouldn't reach completion too but artists from all over Italy flocked to observe and compare the paintings while the great masters worked. The paintings would have defined the style of their times definitely, had they survived.

Leonardo had also gained great respect as an engineer by this time respectively. He was called away by the Florentine government to oversee actual fortifications at Piombino in the midst of his work on the famous Battle of Anghiari.

Leonardo first left Florence for Milan to search of a city where he could be useful as both an engineer and an artist. Ironically he found the lifestyle he had always wanted when he returned back to Florence, at the age of 50.

Back to Milan (1506-1513)

The French governor of Lombardy, Charles d'Amboise, summed Leonardo back to Milan in 1506. He answered the governor's call. However, as an international celebrity now, the artist was in high demand.

The Florentine government sent letter to d'Amboise frequently, asking the French to let Leonardo return to Florence to complete his Battle of Anghiari, which they had paid for. However, Leonardo stayed in Milan, where he had always felt comfortable.

The Confraternity of the Immaculate Conception, which had originally commissioned the *Virgin of the Rocks,* had for a long time been involved in legal battles with the brothers de' Predis, who had painted the side panels. Leonardo had to return to the painting and supervise a new version now. He may have done some work on it too, some experts agree that they see his hand in the angel's face. One can argue that his changing style is seen in the more old and bigger sized Mary.

Leonardo's life took a turn for the good in general. He even became painter and engineer to Louis XII, King of

France. Leonardo met the young Francesco Melzi in 1507 while travelling in the countryside. Melzi was 15 years old at that time. Melzi became one of Leonardo's most beloved student along with Salai.

Leonardo's father died without leaving a will three years ago. And now, his beloved uncle Francesco had died, and had left a large amount to Leonardo. However Leonardo's brothers again tried to cut Leonardo out of his share. This is why Leonardo returned back to Florence, to take his brothers to court. Even the king of France, Louis XII wrote a letter to the court officials in Florence to speed up the legal proceedings. The court lasted for almost six months.

Leonardo increased the effort on his anatomical studies in the meantime. He sketched the every organ in the body, each one from different angles. An extraordinarily modern technique for the sixteenth century. Leonardo also focused himself in the studies of hydraulics.

It was probably his interest in anatomy which led him to an interest in illustrating the myth of Lead and the Swan. In the myth, Zeus assumed the form of a swan in order to seduce and impregnate the beautiful Leda.

Salai was thirty years old when Leonardo met Melzi. Salai was probably jealous of the new boy. The nature of their relationship is unclear but one thing is certain, they became intimate very rapidly.

Leonardo even wrote letters to Melzi while he was in Florence, waiting for the outcome of the court. The letters were written in a casual tone, but he demanded that his letters be answered.

Melzi was much more of a serious student than Salai too. There are several drawings and paintings from Melzi's later years.

As Leonardo aged with every year, he stopped putting out paintings. He focused on his primary interests like science. He had the greatest patronage one could ever hope for too, the king of France. It is certain that he now had more freedom to do whatever he wanted in his time, therefore he pursued his own personal goals even more.

It is also possible that Leonardo spent the greater part of these years working on the Mona Lisa.

Life in Rome (1513-1516)

The Sforza family regained control of Milan in 1512. However the old ruler Ludovico Sforza was long dead and the ruler Maximilian took his place.

Since his old patron was defeated, Leonardo put going to Rome to his mind. In Rome, Leo X, a Medici, was now pope. He went there at the behest of Giuliano de Medici, the popes brother and commander of the papal troops.

With his favorite pupils Salai and Melzi, they stayed in apartments in the Belvedere, a villa inside the walls of the Vatican. Quite a luxury.

Leonardo pursued architecture, hydraulics , the dynamics of mirrors and his other scientific interests during his three years stay in Rome. Medici empire invested quite a lot in dye industry, now their fortune depend on it. In order to aid his patrons, Leonardo tried to make a parabolic solar reflector to speed up the boiling process that is essential to the making of dyes.

Leonardo was also at work on various architectural projects in the meanwhile. However, some experts think that he was still bored. He fancied amusing himself with pranks. According to Vasari, first biographer of Leonardo da Vinci, he was permanently attaching bird wings to a lizard and inflating a pig's intestine so that it filled a room.

Leonardo's notebooks from that time proves us that he was quite interested in hydraulics. He drew several apocalyptic visions, like similar to a biblical flood. The notebooks also contain so many illustrations which combine Leonardo's artistic skills with his interest in hydraulics.

Experts believe that he portrayed himself at this time. It shows an old man with a long beard and haggard look characteristic to Leonardo. If this portrait is indeed a self portrait, as most experts agree, it is remarkable that it is drawn from an angle, not head on. He probably arranged a system of mirrors in order to draw himself from this angle.

Leonardo completed his last major painting while he was still in Rome. The "Saint John the Baptist." The painting is his last and least famous painting. Saint John looked androgynous in the painting and the prudish critics did not appreciate it for centuries.

Saint John the Baptist

It is pretty obvious that this painting is also anatomically incorrect. However, even though Leonardo was making perfect anatomical sketches in his notebooks, he often got anatomy completely wrong in his paintings. No doubt that he looked to science and art from two different windows. Some people also complain that he copied a cheap version of Mona Lisa in this painting.

It is important to note that some people believed Salai modeled for both of those paintings.

Leonardo traveled to Bologna to attend a peace meeting between the Pope and the current king of France of that time, Francis I. Keep in mind that Francis I conquered the Milan upon attaining the throne, however the Medici family wanted him as an ally.

Leonardo constructed a mechanical lion as a peace offering, symbolizing Florence. The lion was able to walk few paces on its own and it opened a trapdoor in his chest to reveal a fleur-de-lis, the symbol of France. As expected, the new King was impressed.

As Vasari mentioned, Leonardo didn't feel very happy in Rome. The pope held him in high esteem, however it is not clear whether the pope or his court granted him much appreciation. They foolishly believed that Leonardo was interested in necromancy, or the conjuring of the recently dead. However the other reason might be that the pope may have had greater interest in other artists such as Michelangelo.

Leonardo spent this period in Rome with a remarkable level of productivity. He consulted in numerous architectural and hydraulic projects. By the time he was about sixty years old, he still didn't stop learning new things. He had his eyes on the properties of mirrors.

France (1516-1519)

Leonardo's patron, also the Pope, Giuliano de Medici died in February of 1516. Leonardo didn't hope to find any great Italian patron at this time, since he had strong opponents such as Michelangelo, Raphael and Titan in Italy. He thought about the invitation Louis XII extended to him first and by Francis I a second time. And he accepted the invitation to move to France and join its rulers in the Loire Valley.

Leonardo, Salai, Melzi and probably one additional servant traveled to the France in three months. They had animals to carry their baggage. Leonardo took all of his belongings, including Mona Lisa with him. He knew he would never come back home again.

Arriving in Amboise, he took up residence in a manor at Cloux, which was connected by a short underground tunnel to the King's château. The King treated him with great honor, as expected.

Leonardo's arm was paralyzed and he could no longer paint. Still, Francis gave him a worthwhile expense to spent. He enjoyed Leonardo's conversation and regarded him the most cultivated man in Europe.

A person with great importance visited Leonardo at Cloux. Don Antonio de Beatis, a secretary to the cardinal of Aragon. Leonardo describes him as a great gentleman.

Leonardo showed de Beatis his notebooks to give Beatis the impression that they would eventually be published. Although Leonardo arranged chapter headings and timetables for treatises on casting, painting, vision, the flight of birds, the voice, ballistics, hydraulics, building materials and human anatomy, none of them were ever completed.

Leonardo composed his will in April of 1519. He wills his soul to "Almighty God." It is a solid sign that if he ever had abandoned his faith, he now returned to religion.

Sforza had granted him a vineyard, which was divided between his servant and Salai. Salai also inherited the house that Leonardo had been paying for him to live in. Leonardo also left his brothers 400 ducats, somehow a decent sum of money. He also left them the property he inherited from his uncle Francesco that he had fought for in court.

He named Melzi as his executor and left him everything else, including all his arts and writings. It wasn't unexpected that Leonardo also wanted an elaborate funeral.

The bastard son of a wealthy man and a peasant, accused of sodomy, deprived from reputation and his home, had now achieved great success, however more he deserved.

The legend died on the second of May. According to Vasari, he gave his last breath in the arms of the King.

PERSONAL RELATIONS

Salai

His real name was Gian Giacomo Caprotti da Oreno. Salai actually meant "Little Devil". As Leonardo himself recorded, Salai entered Leonardo's household around 1490 at the age of 10. Leonardo has recorded his first and second day with Salai as this:

"Giacomo came to live with me on St Mary Magdalene's day (22 July) 1490, aged ten years. The second day I had two shirts cut out for him, a pair of hose and a jerkin, and when I put aside some money to pay for these things he stole the money (4 lire) out of the purse; and I could never make him confess although I was quite certain of it. The day after I went to sup with Giacomo Andrea, and the said Giacomo supped for two and did mischief for four, for he broke three cruets and spilled the wine."

Salai was a lot of things in the eyes of Leonardo. He was an adoptive son, friend, helper, pupil and probably a lover to Leonardo. Vasari described Salai as: " a graceful and beautiful youth with fine curly hair, in which Leonardo greatly delighted."

Their relationship didn't start as smooth as it ended. A year later they met, Leonardo made a list of the boy's wrong doings. Leonardo called him " a thief, a liar, stubborn and a glutton."

The boy stole money and valuables at least 5 times. He also spent a fortune on apparel. For some reason he had twenty four shoes.

Despite all the problems in their relationship, Salai remained da Vinci's loyal companion, servant and assistant for the next twenty nine years until the Leonardo's death. Leonardo's belongings revealed the pictures of a handsome, curly-haired adolescent, quite possibly of Salai.

Leonardo used Salai as a model for a lot of his works. Most famous one is Saint John the Baptist. Every expert pointed out that this is not a conventional presentation of the Baptist.

In the painting, the exotic Salai poses with his feminine face and ringlet curls. He has a mysterious smile and points up and over his shoulder. Some experts believe that the portrait had the cross and fur pelts painted later. It is a possibility that Leonardo drew the Salai as St John the Baptist without clothes. The painting was not a commissioned work either, he pointed the portrait for himself.

Some believe that it was the last painting Leonardo painted and kept with him at all times. People also said that Leonardo hung the portrait alongside the famous Mona Lisa in his bedroom in France.

The painting isn't that famous as other works of Leonardo. However, the look and smile on Salai's face drew the most attention on the painting. His expression on his face and his finger pointing upwards and the meaning behind of it all have survived for five hundred years as one of the greatest mysteries in art history.

Even today, the relationship between da Vinci and Salai is looked over. So few people are willing to talk about this relationship. It is undeniable that Salai was too important in the life of Leonardo to be looked over.

Salai appears in Leonardo's paintings, including erotic drawings. They traveled everywhere together. Salai also inherited half of Leonardo's wealth. When they were alive, critics stated that Salai's work was almost as good as Leonardo's. Today, they say he was not a good artist.

Leonardo saw Salai first when he was drawing in a field and then approached his father to train Salai as his assistant and apprentice. Salai was only a peasant like Leonardo's mother. It is obvious that Leonardo saw some potential in the boy and wanted to give Salai the opportunity to do something great with his life. As Leonardo himself said, he was also incredibly attractive.

Although there is no definite proof exists of Leonardo's homosexuality, there are plenty of indications in his male erotic drawings as well as in his writings that he was attracted to males.

Homosexuality was common in his time. When he was charged with sodomy in his young, there were already 16,000 men implicated in sodomy, of whom almost 3,000 were convicted. The scale is huge if you think that the city only had 40,000 habitants.

Leonardo never married or showed any interest in women in his whole life. One time even, he wrote that male-female intercourse disgusted him. His drawings of anatomical organs shows much more extensive attention to male organs. Leonardo also surrounded himself with beautiful young males, such as Salai and Melzi.

As a young man, Leonardo himself was very attractive too. His first biographer Vasari says: "There is something supernatural in the accumulation in one individual of so much beauty, grace and might. With his right hand he could twist an iron horseshoe as if it were made of lead. In his liberality, he welcomed and gave food to any friend, rich or poor."

His kindness, his sweet nature, his eloquence ("his speech could bend in any direction the most obdurate of wills") his regal magnanimity, his sense of humor, his love of wild creatures, his "terrible strength in argument, sustained by intelligence and memory," the subtlety of his mind "which never ceased to devise inventions," his aptitude for mathematics, science, music, poetry.

To add to all of that, Vasari says that Leonardo was a man of physical beauty beyond compare. Verrocchio himself used Leonardo as a model at the age of fourteen for two of his works. First the bronze statue of David in the Bargello then the Archangel Michael in Tobias and the Angel with his white dog by his feet.

It is also believed that Leonardo painted himself as young man in his unfinished Adoration of the Magi. The man in the lower right corner looking away is believed to be him.

David

Tobias and the Angel

Adoration of the Magi

There is also a new discovered portrait of Leonardo da Vinci in the National Gallery of Art. The painting was painted between 1475 and 1480 and features him and his white dog.

Salai's name appears most in all of Leonardo's notebooks. It also appears as crossed out on the back of an erotic drawing made by Leonardo, The Incarnate

Angel. It is a humorous and revealing take on his major work, Saint John the Baptist.

The Incarnate Angel

Another erotic work, found on the verso of a foglio in the Atlantic Codex, depicts il Salaino's behind, towards which march several penises on two legs. Some of Leonardo's other works on erotic topics, his drawings of heterosexual human sexual intercourse, were destroyed by a priest who found them after his death.

Salai stole things, broke things, lied, and was generally a devil; if he were a mere student or servant he would have been fired. Instead of punishing him Leonardo showered him with finest of clothes–this would have been unusual behavior toward a servant or a pupil.

Salai left France in 1519 when his master died and returned to Milan to work on Leonardo's vineyard, previously worked by Salai's father, which was granted to him by Leonardo's will.

Salaì married Bianca Coldiroli d'Annono on June 14, 1523, at the age of 43. Unfortunately, he died from a wound received from a crossbow in a duel in 1524.

An inventory of his possessions shows that he inherited many works by Leonardo, including the Mona Lisa and the Infant St John the Baptist.

Salai, painted Monna Vanna, the nude version of Mona Lisa in 1515. Art historians states that it is almost certainly based on a lost original by Leonardo. In the painting, the connection between Salai's face and the face in the portraits is very clear. The Monna Vanna has Salai's eyes, distinctive nose, lips, the shape of his face as well as his ringlet curls. The anatomy of the portrait is the anatomy of a man except the breasts. The neck and arms are large, depicting a man's.

Gian Giacomo Caprotti (Salai)'s only signed painting is Head of Christ, painted in 1511. The head of Christ looks just like the head of Salai.

Monna Vanna - Salai

Verrocchio

Verrocchio was Leonardo da Vinci's master. His real name is Andrea di Cione, but people know him as Verrocchio. Verrocchio owned one of the finest workshops in the Florence.

"Verrocchio" means " true eye" in Italian, a tribute given to him for his artistic achievement. He was a successful painter, sculptor, and goldsmith.

Few paintings are attributed to him with certainty, but a number of important painters were trained at his workshop. Pietro Perugino, Lorenzo di Credi and finally the great Leonardo da Vinci were some of the people he taught art in his workshop. His greatest importance was as a sculptor and his last work, the *Equestrian statue of Bartolomeo Colleoni* in Venice, is generally accepted as a masterpiece.

When Leonardo started apprenticing for him, Verrocchio saw great talent in the boy. Even though Leonardo was only a garzone (studio boy) in the workshop, Verrocchio gave him more and more responsibility.

Eventually, he let Leonardo work with him in one of his paintings, The Baptism of Christ. The young angel holding Jesus' robe in a manner that was so far superior to his master's it made Verrocchio put down his brush and never painted again.

When Leonardo reached twenty years old, he qualified as a master in Guild of saint Luke, the guild of artists and doctors of medicine. After that, Leonardo's father set him up his own workshop. But his attachment to Verrocchio was so strong that he continued to collaborate with his master still.

Even though Verrocchio was a great master and thought countless abilities to Leonardo, he failed to teach him wall painting, as he had no knowledge on the subject. He preferred to make statues mostly. This gave a birth to an important issue for Leonardo, since he tried to paint The Last Supper on the wall, but "failed" because he didn't used the right kind of paints for a wall painting.

Machiavelli

Leonardo was one of the best painter, inventor, scientist and engineer and perhaps one of the greatest creative mind in human history. Machiavelli was the mastermind who helped invent modern political science, whose name became synonymous with deceit and manipulation. When these two great person became together, one can only expect wonderful things to happen.

During a war between Florence and Pisa, Machiavelli hired Leonardo to help him steal the Arno River. The Arno River passed through the Florence and continued on to reach the city of Pisa.

By changing the way of the river, they tried to cut up the water resource of Pisa and let it dry. This way, they couldn't get help from their allies from the river when Florence attack Pisa.

According to his blueprints, Leonardo would have irrigated the entire Arno River Valley with canals, locks and dams, rerouting all the water directly to Florence and leave the Pisa to dry out.

However, the plan was too advanced for 16th century technology. The channels dug to divert the river were too shallow. When they tried to make the channels deeper, a storm destroyed its walls, killing some of the workers and prompting others to get out of the canal.

Even though the joint effort of this two remarkable men was unsuccessful, it led both of them to greatest work of their time. The missed opportunity pushed Machiavelli to leave politics and write one of the most influential pieces of literature from the Renaissance: The Prince. Leonardo came out winning too. The river on the background in his most famous painting, Mona Lisa, is Arno River itself. Leonardo chose to draw that river, since he knew it well enough to obsess over it. Even long after the plot with Machiavelli failed.

Michelangelo

Vasari states that Michelangelo and Leonardo felt an intense dislike for each other, although he doesn't specify a reason. However, there is an interesting story from an anonymous manuscript called the Codice Magliabecchiano. It goes like this:

"As Leonardo, accompanied by [his friend] Giovanni di Gavina, was passing the Spini Bank, near the church of Santa Trinità, several notables were assembled who were discussing a passage in Dante and seeing Leonardo, they asked him to come and explain it to them.

At the same moment Michelangelo passed and, one of the crowd calling to him, Leonardo said: 'Michelangelo will be able to tell you what it means.' To which Michelangelo, thinking this had been said to entrap him, replied: 'No, explain it yourself, horse-modeller that you are, who, unable to cast a statue in bronze, were forced to give up the attempt in shame.' So saying, he turned his back on them and left. Leonardo remained silent and blushed at these words."

Leonardo's intentions were unclear, but he knew that Michelangelo was into Dante at the time. Some critics say that he only wanted to benefit from his knowledge of Dante. Some say Michelangelo was jealous of Leonardo.

It all started when they were commissioned to paint the walls of Council Hall. Some can say that it was a point-scoring competition between two geniuses as Leonardo and Michelangelo. Leonardo was commissioned in 1503, when he was in his early fifties. By this time, he had just painted the famous Mona Lisa. Vasari says that "His fame had so increased, that all persons who took delight in art - nay, the whole city of Florence - desired that he should leave them some memorial work."

Leonardo was commissioned to paint a vast wall painting of The Battle of Anghiari, a scene from the 15th-century wars between Florence and Milan. Then, in December 1504, a far younger Florentine was commissioned to paint The Battle of Cascina, which took place between Florence and Pisa in the 14th century, on the same wall of the Council Hall.

Michelangelo was just a prodigy at the time, 29 years old. He had born in 1475 and trained in the sculpture academy created by Lorenzo de Medici in a garden in Florence. He had carved the Pieta in St Peter's in Rome by 1498, in May 1504, the same month that Leonardo revised his contract with the Signoria of Florence to put back the completion date of The Battle of Anghiari,

Michelangelo's statue of David was installed outside the Palazzo Vecchio. Leonardo, inconceivably, had a rival.

Vasari explained clearly that this was indeed a contest between the two. He says that Michelangelo was commissioned in competition with Leonardo. However the same competition opened other doors to powerful emotions such as paranoia, hatred. According to Vasari, Michelangelo made his dislike for Leonardo so clear that Leonardo left for France just to avoid him. Leonardo made remarks in his notebooks on the "wooden" qualities of Michelangelo's paintings.

It is obvious that Piero Soderini had mischief in his mind when he set Leonardo and Michelangelo to work on the same wall. Not surprisingly, what happened in the Palazzo Vecchio turned out to be more mysterious and more private to both these artists than anyone expected.

It was more than an artistic rivalry. The council hall was the centre of a new idea of the Florentine Republic. The hall was restored with a far greater commitment than ever after the expulsion of the Medici in 1494. It basically represented the whole city and the people in it. The rebirth of the Florentine Republic was a moment of intense self-rediscovery for Florence; after a century in which the city had become more like a conventional princedom, it was reasserting republican government.

Brilliant minds of the time gave their all the to the struggle to recreate the Republic.

Machiavelli was one of Piero Soderini's close allies. As some of the historians used to believe, Machiavelli played a huge hand in commissioning Leonardo to decorate the Council Hall.

One thing was certain. Both Leonardo and Michelangelo had new hope for their city. They had been working far from their home, in Milan, in Rome. However once more, they felt the warm and welcoming air of their city.

The city of Florence would be the winner no matter what, having new patriotic masterpieces as the result of the rivalry that would spur two greatest artist of the time. The rivalry spurred them but in an odd, pessimistic directions. The images of war they created were not bright and celebratory pageants of chivalry, but enigmatic, disturbing.

Leonardo and Michelangelo were very different from each other. Different ages, different styles. Leonardo favored a more soft, shadowy, ambiguous style while Michelangelo chose more of a sublimely decisive kind. But they both had one thing in common. Neither of them liked to finish anything. Everyone in the city of Florence knew this already when Leonardo was commissioned to paint the Council Hall. But no one knew that Michelangelo, who had been prodigious, was to become dilatory and difficult. Michelangelo's abortive work on The Battle of Cascina marks the beginning of the pattern of non-completion that continued his whole life. One can even say that he learned this from Leonardo.

Surprisingly, Leonardo got a lot further than Michelangelo this time. From the sketches of men and horses that survived, we can conclude how passionately he engaged with it. The horses as tense and confrontational as the men, the men as bestial as the animals. Warriors had their mouths snarlingly open in the Battle of Anghiari, as if they wanted to bite the flesh of their enemies.

Leonardo used his remarkable engineering talent while painting. He built a wooden elevator so he could move up and down the wall in comfort. However he made a mistake as he did with the Last Supper. Leonardo learned about a method based on a recipe in the ancient Roman writer Pliny the Elder. The recipe apparently would enable him to paint the wall in oils. However as expected, the recipe didn't work, leaving the upper part dried dark and the lower parts disintegrated.

The promising prodigy, Michelangelo never got past the drawing stage. But it was still the most remarkable drawing in the eyes of the people. After taking over a room in the Hospital of Dyers in Florence, he drew a full sized cartoon in large detail. The drawing was very startling.

Unlike Leonardo who depicted the heart of battle in an agonizing, horrific entanglement of human and animal bodies, Michelangelo drew war's margins, a moment of bizarre ordinariness. In the drawing, Florentine soldiers hear the enemy coming and rush to get out of water and put on armor when bathing naked in the famous Arno river.

As the result, once can agree that Leonardo won the "competition." His painting reached the wall, unlike Michelangelo's, whose painting remained as a drawing. Leonardo's painting was painted over in 1565 by Vasari, Leonardo's first biographer, for the unknown reasons.

Melzi

Francesco Melzi was a son of an aristocrat that met Leonardo when he was 15 and stayed with him almost his entire life. Leonardo met Melzi when he was wandering the country side in France.

Melzi, described Leonardo's feelings towards him with his own words in a letter: "sviscerato et ardentissimo amore" *meaning* " a deeply passionate and most burning love".

When Leonardo first brought Melzi with himself, Salai became extremely jealous as expected. After all, he was the Leonardo's favorite until Melzi arrived. But Leonardo did what he can to keep Salai happy.

Salai accepted Melzi's presence eventually and all three of them lived together after that. They went into countless adventures throughout Italy. Eventually, Melzi became Leonardo's pupil and life companion. It is also widely believed that Melzi was Leonardo's favorite student.

Melzi accompanied Leonardo on trips to Rome in 1513 and to France in 1517. Melzi worked closely with and for Leonardo as a painter. Some of the works that attributed to Leonardo later attributed to Melzi.

It was Melzi who inherited the artistic and scientific works, manuscripts and collections of Leonardo after his master's death. After Leonardo's death, Melzi returned to Italy. He married and fathered a son in there named Orazio. However, when Orazio died on his estate in Vaprio d'Adda, his heirs sold the collection of Leonardo's works.

INVENTIONS
Anemometer

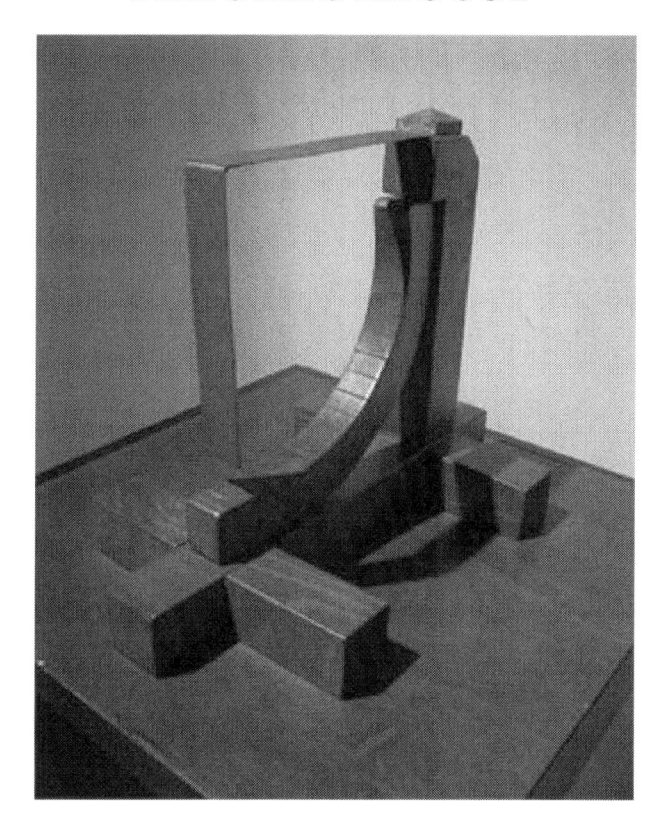

Anemometer

An **anemometer** is a device used for measuring wind speed, and is a common weather station instrument. The term is derived from the Greek word anemos, which means wind, and is used to describe any wind speed measurement instrument used in meteorology.

Some historians think that Leonardo's fascination with flight led him to innovate the anemometer. He hoped to learn the direction of the wind before attempting to flight eventually.

However, it is now known that the original device was invented by Leon Batista in 1450 and Leonardo made variations on the existing design between 1483-1486. He made it easier to measure wind force.

Next to his sketches of the anemometer, da Vinci made the following notes: "For measuring distance traversed per hour with the force of the wind. Here a clock for showing time is required."

Leonardo's anemometer had a kind of irregular shape for a device like that. It had an arched frame with a rectangular piece of wood hanging in the center by a hinge. The piece of wood inside the arched frame raises when the wind blows. There was a scale printed on the frame. And a person could measure the force of the wind by noting the highest point that the wood reach on the scale.

Flying Machine

Leonardo da Vinci's favorite area of study was the area of aviation. Ever since the time a bird landed on him as a baby, Leonardo wanted for himself and all the mankind to be able to fly.

One of da Vinci's most famous inventions, the flying machine (also known as the "ornithopter") ideally displays his powers of observation and imagination, as well as his enthusiasm for the potential of flight. Da Vinci hoped to replicate the flight of winged animals for this design. In his notes, he indicates that bats, kites and birds are his sources of inspiration.

The inspiration of the bat shines through the most, as the two wings of the device feature pointed ends commonly associated with the winged creature. Leonardo da Vinci's flying machine had a wingspan that exceeded 33 feet, and the frame was to be made of pine covered in raw silk to create a light but sturdy membrane.

The pilot needed to lie face down in the center of the invention on a board. The pilot would pedal a crank connected to a rod and pulley system to power the wings. Aiming an increased output on the machine, it also had a hand crank also a head piece for steering. The wings of the machine clap as the pilot spins the cranks with his hands and feet. The inspiration of nature in the invention is apparent in the way the wings were designed to twist as they flapped.

Unfortunately, as da Vinci probably realized, while the flying machine may have flown once it was in the air, a person could never have created enough power to get the device off the ground. It could work when you jump off a high cliff or tower.

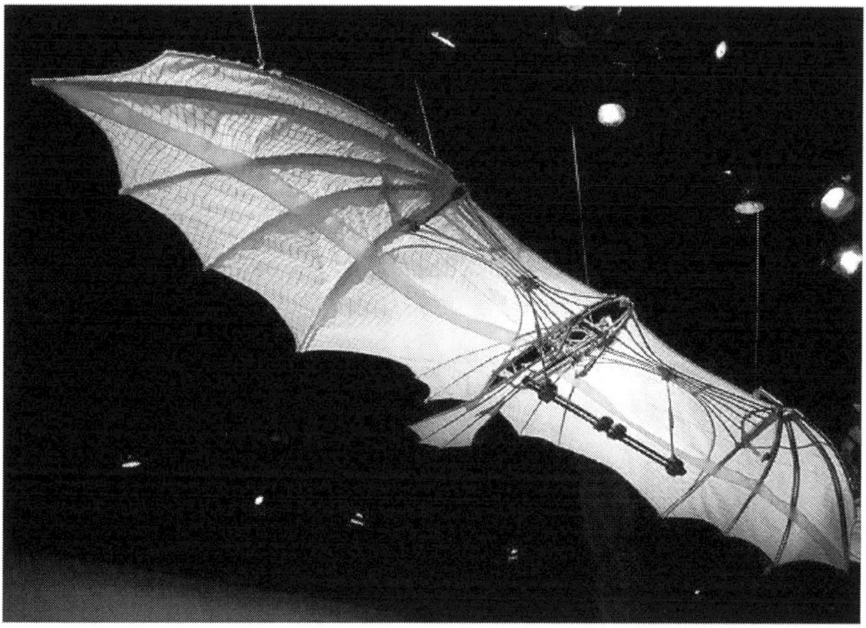

Helicopter

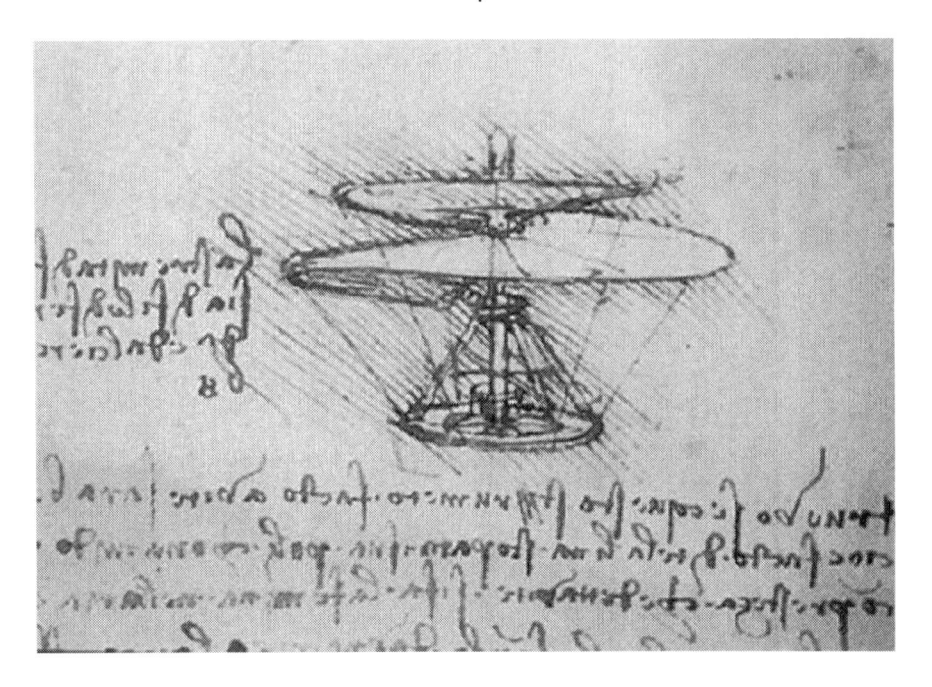

Even though the first actual helicopter built in the 1940s, it is believed that Leonardo da Vinci's sketches from the late fifteenth century were the predecessor to the modern day flying machine. As characteristic to the Leonardo, he never actually built and tested it. But in his notes and drawings, he mapped out exactly how the device would operate.

Da Vinci scrawled next to his sketches of the screw-like machine the following description: "If this instrument made with a screw be well made – that is to say, made of linen of which the pores are stopped up with starch and be turned swiftly, the said screw will make its spiral in the air and it will rise high."

The device is also known as the "Helical Air Screw" or simply the "airscrew". The device would compress the air to obtain flight, very similar to today's helicopters. Da Vinci saw the potential of the screw shape in other areas as well, as he used the shape for other inventions and designs too.

Leonardo's helicopter measured more than 15 feet in diameter and was made from reed, linen and wire. Four men would power it by standing on a central platform turning cranks to rotate the shaft. Leonardo believed that the device would lift off the ground with enough rotation. However, modern scientist don't believe that the famous invention would not have been able to take flight due to weight constrictions.

Parachute

The modern day parachute was invented by Sebastien Lenormand in 1783. However, as the great genius he is, Leonardo conceived the parachute idea a few hundred years earlier.

Leonardo made a sketch of the invention with this accompanying description: "If a man have a tent made of linen of which the apertures (openings) have all been stopped up, and it be twelve braccia (about 23 feet) across and twelve in depth, he will be able to throw himself down from any great height without suffering any injury."

The most distinct aspect of Leonardo's parachute design was that the canopy was triangular rather than rounded. This lead many scientist to question whether it would actually have enough air resistance to float. Also, da Vinci design the invention so that it had a linen covering a wood frame. The hefty weight of the device would also present another problem.

The idea itself never actually built or tested by Leonardo himself. However, in 2000, a man named Adrian Nicholas constructed a prototype based on da Vinci's design and tested it. Against all the claims, Leonardo's design worked as intended. Nichols even said that it had a smoother ride than the modern parachute.

33-Barreled Organ

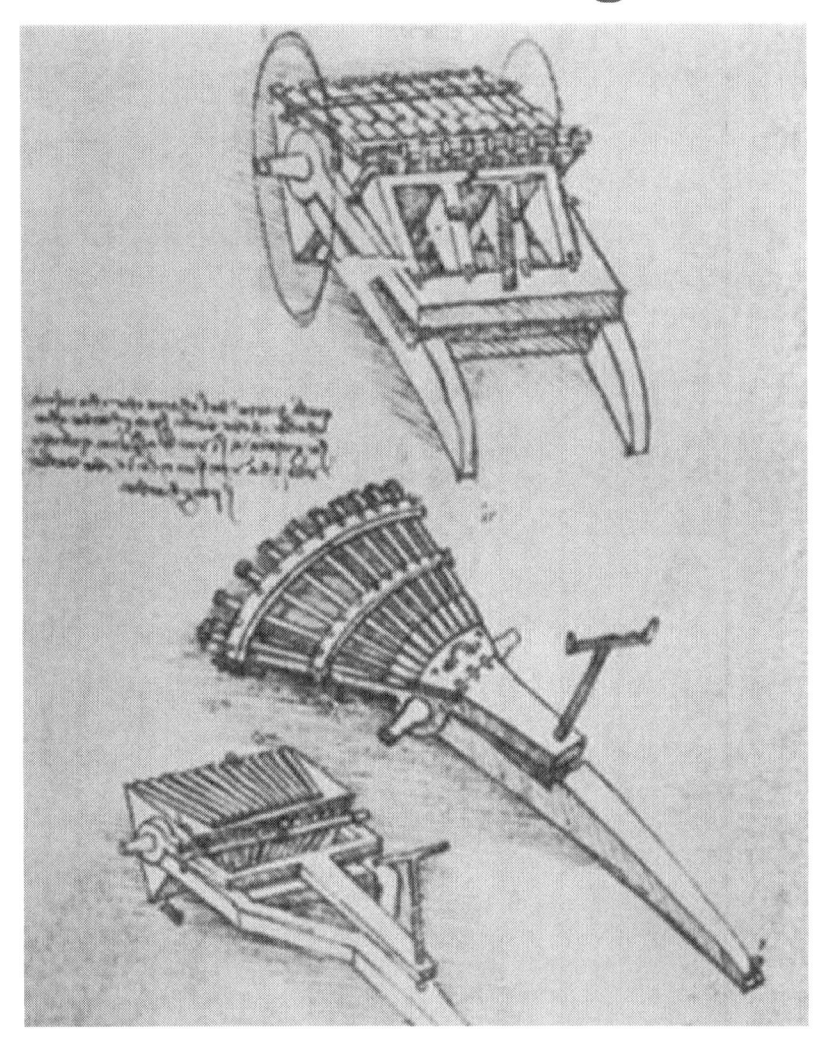

As Leonardo himself noted, the problem with the canons of the time was that they took far too long to load. His solution to that problem was to build multi-barreled guns that could be loaded and fired simultaneously.

The idea featured 33 small-caliber guns connected together. The canons were divided into three rows of 11 guns each, all connected to a single revolving platform. There are two large wheels attached to the sides of the platform, making it mobile.

All the guns on the organ would be loaded and then, during battle, the first row of 11 would be fired. The platform would then be rotated to properly aim the next row of canons. The idea was that while one set of canons was being fired, another set would be cooling and the third set could be loaded. This system allowed soldiers to repeatedly fire without interruption.

The reason that the weapon is called organ is that the rows of canon barrels resemble the pipes of an organ. Leonardo's famous design generally regarded as the basis for the modern day machine gun. The modern day machine gun didn't really develop for use until the 19th century.

Tank-Armored Car

Almost like a prototype to the modern tanks, Leonardo's armored car was equipped with lots of weapons and was capable of moving in any direction. It is the most famous war machine invention of Leonardo. The armored car was designed to intimidate and scatter the opposing army. It doesn't seem like much in today's conditions but back in the day, a huge armored car approaching you while you only have a sword in hand is very scary.

Leonardo's vehicle has a number of light cannons arranged on a circular platform with wheels that allow for 360-degree range. The platform is covered by a large protective cover (like the shell of a turtle), reinforced with metal plates, which was to be slanted to better deflect enemy fire. There is a sighting turret on top to coordinate the firing of the cannons and the steering of the vehicle.

The eight men inside the tank would have to constantly turn the cranks to spin the wheels of the machine. In his notes Leonardo stated that he also thought of using horses to move the machine but then he dismissed it by saying that horses would become too unpredictable in the confines of the tank during a battle.

Despite its elaborate design, Leonardo's tank has a major flaw - the powering cranks went in opposite directions. This made forward motion impossible. Scholars suggest such a basic engineering flaw would never have escaped the detail-oriented mind of Leonardo da Vinci, and that he may have inserted the flaw intentionally. A pacifist at heart, Leonardo might have sabotaged his own design to discourage the war machine from every being built.

Giant Crossbow

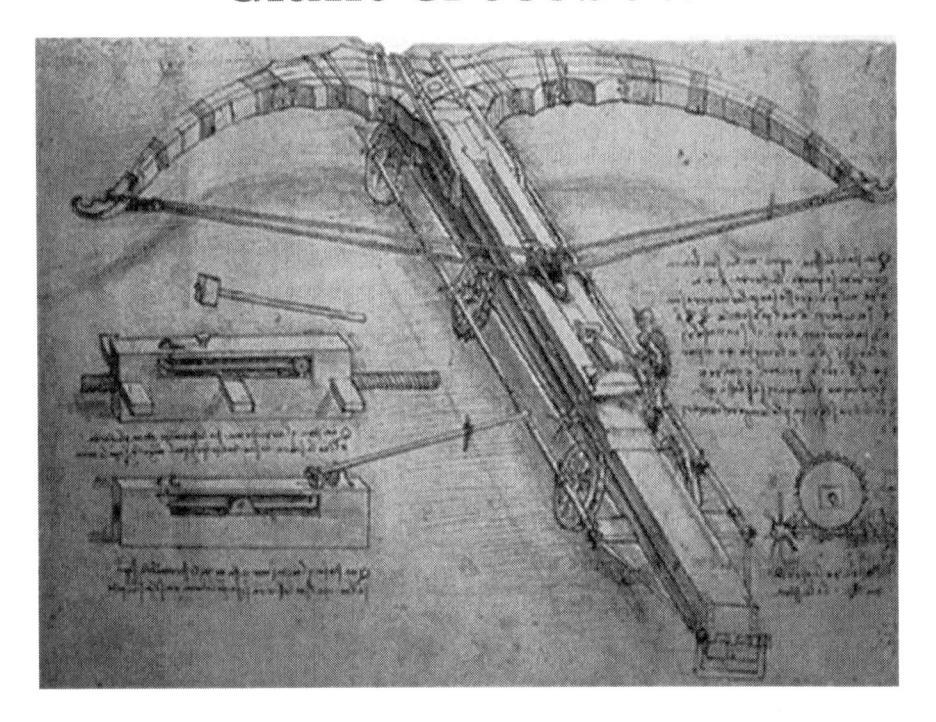

One of the feature that makes Leonardo different from others is that he knew the power of psychological effects of weapons in warfare. Leonardo knew that the fear weapons could instill in enemies was just as important than the damage they could inflict, if not more so.

This is why Leonardo designed devices so he can affect his enemies psychologically. This giant crossbow, was the result of this idea. Designed for pure intimidation, Leonardo's crossbow was to measure 42 braccia or 27 yards across. For the mobility, the device had three wheels on each side. The bow itself would be made of thin wood for flexibility.

However, contrary to normal crossbow, Leonardo did not design this crossbow so it could fire giant arrows. He designed it so that it can fire large stones or possibly flaming bombs even. To use the device, a soldier spins a crank to pull back the bow and loads the artillery. The soldier would then use a mallet to knock out a holding pin and fire the weapon.

However improbable, Leonardo made the ideas look realistic and plausible in his notebooks. One can think that even if it wasn't an efficient way to fight with enemies, he design the machine so he can terrify enemies into fleeing rather than fighting.

Triple Barrel Canon

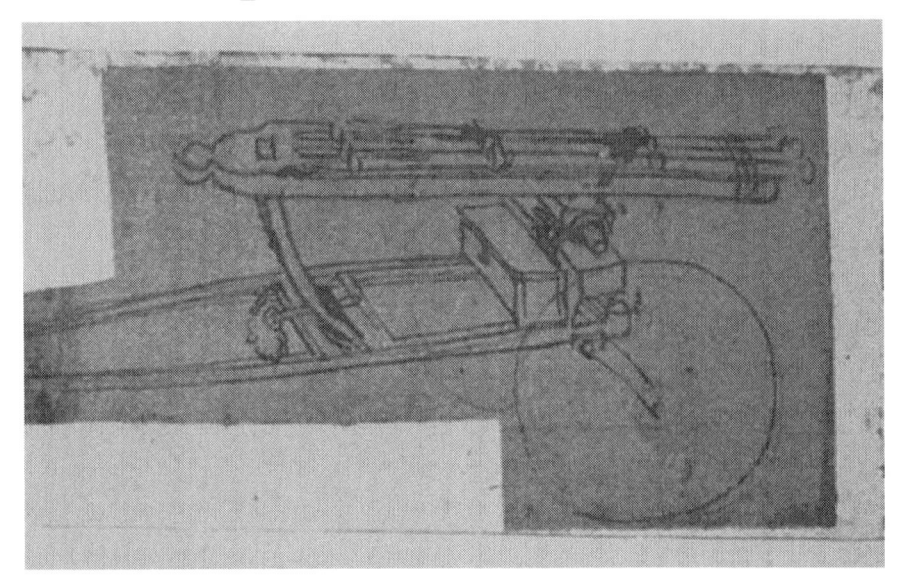

Leonardo believed that mobility was a crucial necessity to victory on the battlefield. This is what made him great as a military engineer, he saw what was needed to win. This idea is seen in many of his war inventions such as his mobile bridges and ladders to many of his weapon designs. Triple Barrel Canon is a prime example of the idea.

When da Vinci was alive, since they were heavy and took a lot of time to reload, cannons were generally used at home in stationary positions rather than on the battlefield. Leonardo designed his triple barrel canon to solve both of these problems – a fast and light weapon that could do a lot of damage on the battlefield.

The design featured three thin canons that would be front-loaded and adjustable in height. Unlike a traditional canon, where one shot would be fired before reloading, da Vinci's canon allowed soldiers to load three shots at once, enabling them to fire more frequently. The lighter weight and large wheels allowed the gun carriage to be moved around to different areas during battle.

Leonardo was a genius who predicted, maybe altered the future. The gunpowder was in its infancy during the 15th century, but Leonardo used it frequently in his designs. The actual emergence of the gunpowder as the weapon of choice was only in 19th and 20th century.

Clock

Leonardo didn't just invented more machines. He also improved some of the devices that were invented before him, such as clock. He didn't reinvent it but he designed a more accurate clock.

While clocks that showed hours and minutes had become increasingly accurate in Leonardo's time, they didn't really make a big leap forward until the incorporation of the pendulum about two hundred years later.

Leonardo's clock had two separate mechanisms: one for minutes and one for hours. Each was made up of elaborately connected weights, gears and harnesses. The clock also has a dial for keeping track of moon phases.

Leonardo's major innovation was to have springs, rather than weights operate his clock. He also included the detail of some materials that would be used to make the clock – including diamonds and rocks.

Colossus

Perhaps even more interesting than the ambition and innovation behind Leonardo da Vinci's Colossus invention is the heartbreaking story of his attempts to bring it to life. Typically, you would expect Leonardo to stop working on a project. However this time, he didn't want to stop. He really wanted to build this giant bronze horse for Milan, but fate did not allow him.

In 1482, the Duke of Milan commissioned Leonardo to build the largest horse statue in the world. Leonardo, never afraid of a challenge designed a 24-foot bronze statue, and then went to work creating a clay model. The next step was to cover the model in bronze – not an easy task.

Because of the size of the statue, it required 80 tons of bronze, which had to be applied in an even thickness or the statue would be unstable. To do this Leonardo used his experience in designing canons to invent a whole new mold-making technique. He also had to invent an innovative oven to reach the temperature needed to heat such a large amount of bronze.

After finally solving all of the design problems that confronted him Leonardo was ready for bronzing. Unfortunately, fate intervened, and, in 1494, King Charles invaded France. To hold off the French army, the Duke offered a bribe of Leonardo's bronze – which the French ultimately used to make canons. The last thing Leonardo wrote about the Colossus was: "I will speak of the horse no more."

A retired airline pilot and artist from Pennsylvania named Charles Dent decided the revive the Colossus project in 1977. He set up a non-profit organization to do it. He spent the next 17 years working on it before dying in 1994. Finally, in 1999, the horse was completed and given as a gift to the people of Milan, Italy.

Ideal City

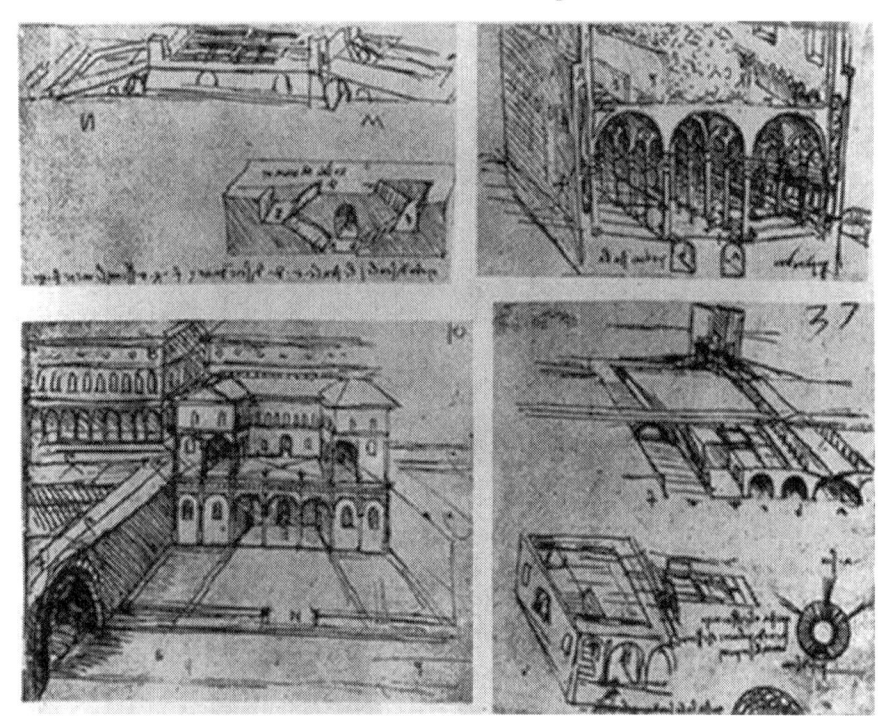

Nothing reflects the epic ambition and scope of Leonardo da Vinci's inventions better than his ideal city. The invention combines Leonardo's talents as an artist, architect, engineer and inventor to create an entire city.

The idea came to the Leonardo after the plague had ravaged Milan, killing almost a third of the city's population. Thus, Leonardo wanted to design a city that would be more united, with greater communications, services and sanitation to prevent the future spread of diseases.

His ideal city combined a series of connected canals, which would be used for commercial purposes and as sewage system. The city would future lower areas, canals for tradesmen and travelers, and upper areas, roads for gentleman. The street of the Milan were very narrow in those times, causing people to jamming together. As a response, this ideal city's roads were designed to be very broad.

As an artist, one can expect from Leonardo to design a city that features a great vision to behold, with elegant buildings featuring large arches and pillars. Leonardo said of his style of urban planning: "Only let that which is good looking be seen on the surface of the city."

Leonardo detailed many other great and small aspects of his city. These include special stables for horses which the animal loving Leonardo saw as integral to the workings of the city, fresh air vents in buildings. And of course, since Leonardo's design was so grand in scale and required an entire city rebuilt, his ideal city never actually came to life.

Robotic Knight

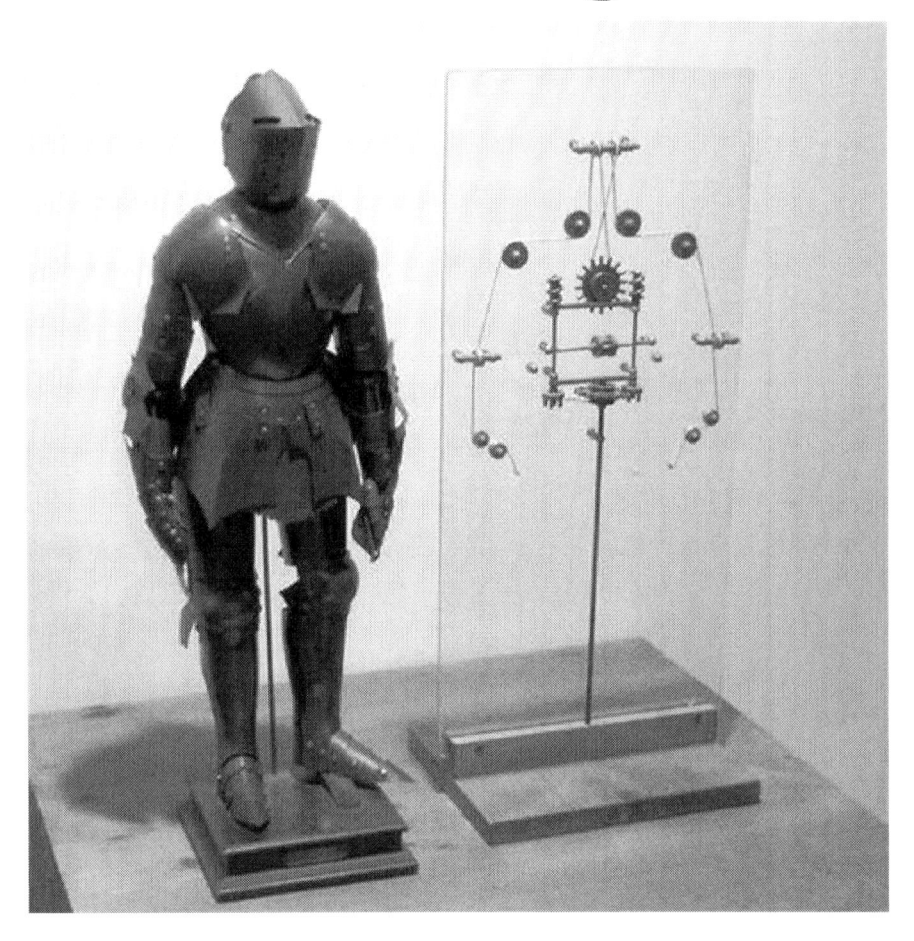

As an engineer, the use of pulleys, weights and gears were crucial components for Leonardo. This is why he used this three components in almost all of his automated designs, including clock, air conditioner and hydraulic power saw.

Leonardo also incorporated these mechanisms into his self-propelled cart invention, which many people consider the very first robot. But Leonardo used the parts to create another robot too – his Robotic Knight. Though a full drawing of Leonardo's robotic knight has never been recovered, fragments detailing different aspects of the knight have been found scattered throughout his notebooks.

The robotic knight was designed for a pageant in Milan which the Duke had put Leonardo in charge of overseeing. It consisted of a knight suit filled with gears and wheels that were connected to an elaborate pulley and cable system. Through these mechanisms, Leonardo's knight was capable of independent motion such as sitting down, standing up, moving its head and lifting its visor.

Roboticist Mark Rosheim built a prototype of the robotic knight in 2002 by using several different da Vinci drawings as blueprints. The robot he built was able to walk and wave. He also stated that Leonardo designed the robotic knight in such a way that it could be easily constructed, without a single unnecessary part.

Self-Propelled Cart

Leonardo da Vinci designed a self-propelled cart capable of moving without being pushed that lead many people into thinking the invention to be the world's first robot.

It was one of the many inventions that da Vinci created dealing with locomotion and transportation. However, historians later come into the conclusion that da Vinci specifically designed the cart for theatrical use.

Leonardo's cart was powered by coiled springs and it also featured steering and brake capabilities. When the brake was released, the car would propel forward, and the steering was programmable to go either straight or at pre-set angles.

Leonardo's cart design was so ahead of its time that its exact workings baffled scholars until late in the 20th century. But, in 2006, Italy's Institute and Museum of the History of Science in Florence built a working model based on da Vinci's design and, to the surprise of many, the cart actually worked. Some experts even noted that it looked similar to the Mars Land Rover.

Scuba Gear

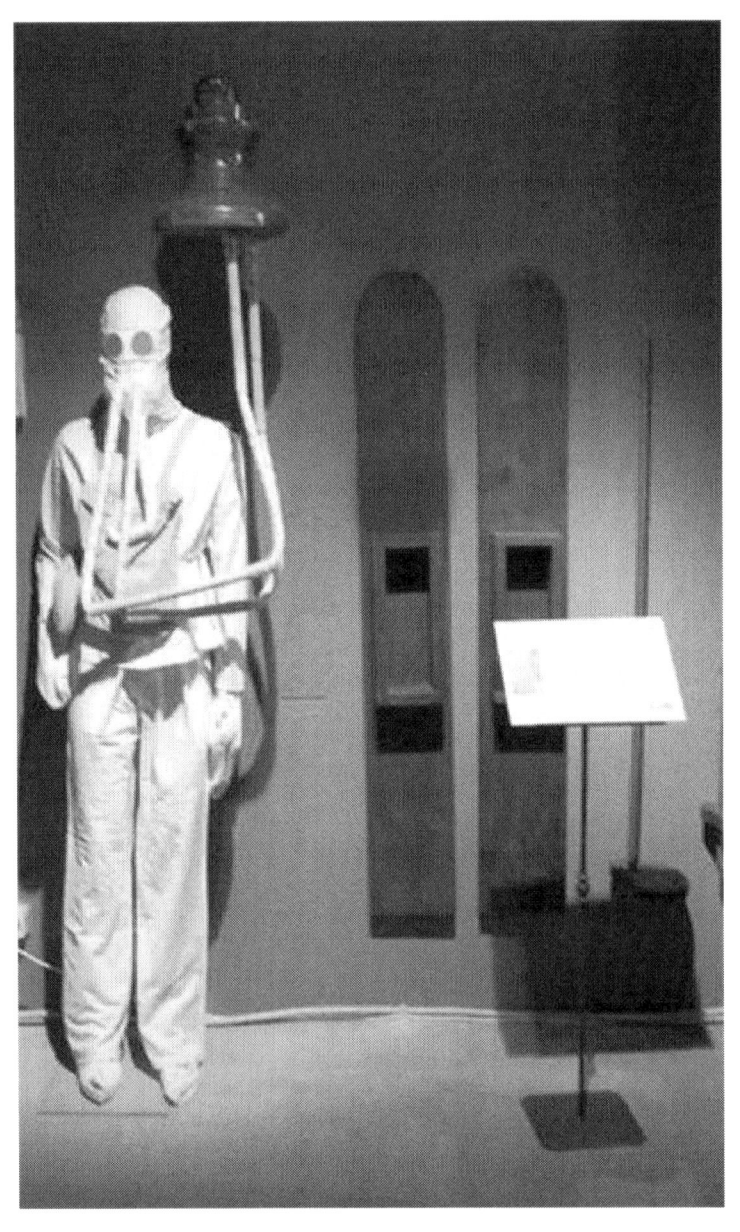

Leonardo's fascination with the world around him made him both a great artist and a great inventor. His fascination did not end with the air and flying, it spilled over to swimming and water too. Leonardo designed many inventions that dealt with water in his lifetime.

In 1500, Leonardo designed his scuba gear for sneak attacks on enemy Ottoman ships from underwater while working in Venice. The leather diving suit was equipped with a bag-like mask that went over the diver's head. Two cane tubes were attached to the mask around the nose that led up to a cork diving bell floating on the surface.

Opening of the tubes provided that air necessary for the diver below. To make the diver be able to easily surface or sink, the mask was equipped with a valve-operated balloon that could be inflated or deflated. Also, da Vinci's scuba gear invention had a pouch for the diver to urinate in.

Despite all of his efforts to win the war, Venetian ruling court did not trust the da Vinci with his invention so the design never reached the surface.

Revolving Bridge

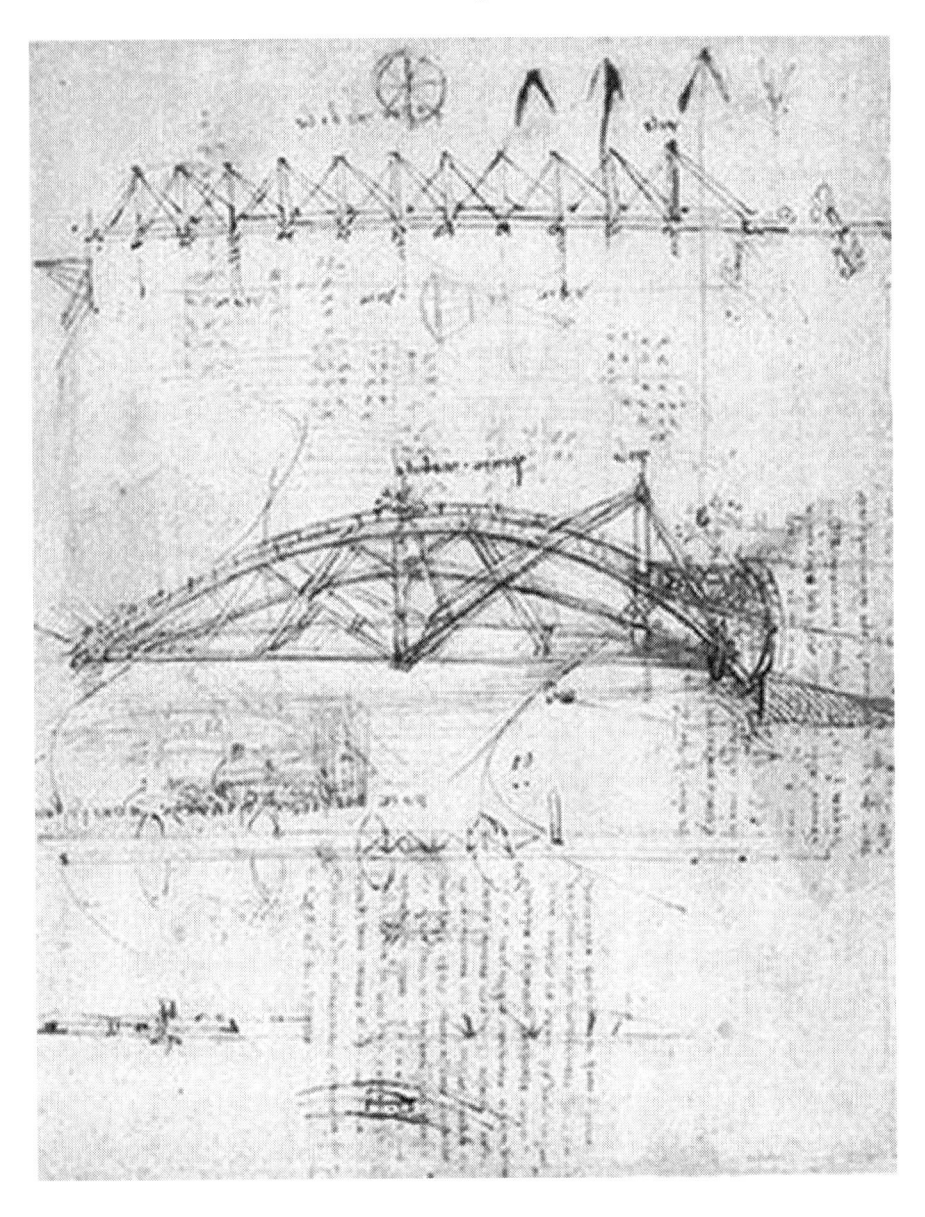

Leonardo designed the revolving bridge for Duke Sforza of the Milan. The bridge could be quickly packed up and transported for use by armies on the move to pass over bodies of water.

Soldiers could pass with little to no trouble when the bridge would swing across a stream or moat and set down on the other side. For both quick employment and easy transport, the invention had wheels and contained a rope and pulley system. For balancing purposes, the bridge was equipped with a counterweight tank.

Da Vinci described the bridge in his notes as being "light yet rugged" and it was one of several bridges he designed for the Duke in his lifetime. Another, similar bridge Leonardo da Vinci built for armies was a fast-construction bridge that made it quicker and easier for soldiers to cross multiple rivers.

Such temporary bridges helped armies to navigate unfamiliar terrain with less difficulty, and more easily escape from pursuing forces. They also provided armies with what da Vinci believed was one of the most important aspects of warfare: mobility.

The Ball Bearing

Leonardo designed the ball bearing to lower the friction between two plates that would be in contact in his other designs such as the aerial screw- also known as helicopter.

Unfortunately, his helicopter would never have flown as humans do not have anywhere near the power to weight ratio necessary to lift themselves against the force of gravity.

A ball bearing is made with smooth spheres put in between surfaces to reduce friction and continue locomotion. The principle behind its workings is really simple, but as with most simple things it is one of the most useful things in the world today. The ball bearings have been present since the ancient and old days of Egypt and Rome, however Leonardo improved the design so that it was the most practical and closest to what a ball bearing is now.

Most of us don't notice how frequently we use ball bearings in real life. They are found in mechanical and electrical devices such as computers, bicycles, stools, hot tubs, washing machines and even game controllers. Many useful things wouldn't function without the ball bearing.

Cluster Bomb

To make the bombard, or cannon, a weapon already known at the time, even more deadly, Da Vinci also designed large projectiles, comprised of round shells fitted around iron spacers and stitched inside a pliable casing. Once fired, this invention exploded into many fragments with that had greater range and impact than a single cannon-ball.

Leonardo da Vinci was fascinated and involved with the concept and design of military machines and devices throughout his whole life. This burning desire led him to this particular invention, making defense of a castle or town significantly easier for the defender.

Instead of having a big army to defend the castle, this cannon could have been used as a mechanism of offence together with a smaller army, defending the premises.

Te cannon he designed was meant to scatter enemies and deliver "splash" damage.

Scythed Chariots

There is a saying that everything you do in a battlefield to survive and win the battle is justified. And this device just proves that.

As Leonardo's beautiful sketches reveal, the device would consist of carriages covered with sharp, swirling blades that moved in the thick of battle, slashing through everything they stumble across.

The rotating blades were specifically designed to sever the limbs of the victims it came across in the battlefield. A soldier would ride the horse that is connected with the carriage behind. The rotating blades were in front of the horse, connected to the carriage behind with two sticks on both sides.

The carriage had two blades on the both sides of it, ready to slash the enemies they encounter. Finally, two huge blades were fitted on the back vertically, rotating simultaneously with the blades in front.

But there was a drawback. The blades didn't chose who they sliced. In one of his drawings, Leonardo illustrated the carnage in such gruesome detail that his notation indicated that his contraption probably would wreak as much havoc on friends as on foes.

Fortress

Leonardo designed this fortress with the idea of keeping those who live inside safe from an attack. The detailed shape is innovative and presumably could have been an effective defense against the impact of deadly artillery projectiles.

The da Vinci fortress could be considered by many as very modern in its design because it had circular towers and the slightly inclined exterior walls designed to absorb attacks from firearms.

The lord of the castle would live in the centre of the complex, the safest place possible, which according to original drawings also had a secret underground passage.

The fortress also features two levels of concentric walls, the tops of which are rounded in order to help deflect the impact of cannon fire. To return fire with minimum risk of injury from the outside, small openings were present at the walls.

ART WORK

Annunciation

The archangel Gabriel is kneeling as a dignified profile figure and raising his right hand in greeting to Mary, indicating her divine pregnancy. The Virgin has stopped reading and reacts to the Annunciation with an expression of deep respect and by gesturing with her left hand. There is a conspicuous perspectival mistake: her right arm had to be painted too long proportionally, so that, despite her seated position, it would still be able to depict the impressive position other hand over the prie-dieu.

Leonardo depicted Mary in a three-quarter profile in front of the corner of a room. All three spatial coordinates - height, width and depth - converge on this point, thus creating a sense of depth in the picture as well as enhancing the importance of Mary. Her head clearly contrasts with the dark wall and her body is emphatically framed by the cornerstones whose parallel lines are converging on her.

The work came to the Uffizi in 1867 from the monastery of San Bartolomeo of Monteoliveto, near Florence. It was ascribed to Domenico Ghirlandaio until 1869, when some critics recognised it as a youthful work by Leonardo, executed around 1472-1475, when he was still an apprentice in the workshop of his master, Andrea del Verrocchio. The sacred scene is set in the garden of a Florentine palace, with a landscape on the background which is already peculiarly Leonardesque, for the magic and unreal atmosphere created by mountains, water and sky. Leonardo's personality is pointed out also in the beautiful drapery of the Virgin and the Angel, while the marble table in front of her probably quotes the tomb of Piero and Giovanni dei Medici in the church of San Lorenzo sculpted by Verrocchio in this period.

Verrocchio used lead-based paint and heavy brush strokes. He left a note for Leonardo to finish the background and the angel. Leonardo used light brush strokes and no lead. When the Annunciation was x-rayed, Verrocchio's work was evident while Leonardo's angel was invisible.

The product of a collaborative efforts in Verrocchiio's studio, this picture is nonetheless a masterful achievement and proof of Leonardo da Vinci's innate pictorial talent. Everything in this work is of a high poetic and stylistic quality: the handling of the figures and their attributes, the spatial construction, and the distant trees and watercourse, which attest to the artist's enduring love of nature. Many changes were to come in his painting, for Leonardo da Vinci was a tireless innovator, but this picture would suffice to rank him among the greatest.

The Baptism of Christ

The Baptism of Christ is a painting finished around 1475 by the Italian Renaissance painter Andrea del Verrocchio and Leonardo da Vinci and his workshop. It is housed in the Uffizi Gallery in Florence.

Commissioned by the monastery church of San Salvi in Florence, where it remained until 1530, the painting was painted in the workshop of Andrea del Verrocchio, whose style is well defined by the figures of Christ and Baptist. The special fame of the work is due to the pupil who helped him paint it. The blond angel on the left and parts of the landscape background belong to the hand of the very young Leonardo da Vinci, who was in Verrocchio's workshop around 1470. Some critics ascribe the second angel to another young Florentine artist, Sandro Botticelli.

The painting portrays St. John the Baptist baptizing Jesus by pouring water over his head. The extended arms of God, the golden rays, the dove with outstretched wings, and the cruciform nimbus show that Jesus is the Son of God and part of the Trinity. Two angels on the riverbank are holding Jesus' garment. The composition as a whole is attributed to Verrocchio, as master and head of the workshop, and large parts of the painting are considered his work.

Leonardo was 23 at the time it was painted and part of his contribution was the angel holding the mantle. The kneeling figure already shows signs of characteristics Leonardo would retain and develop throughout the rest of his career, particularly in the luminous tumbling locks of hair, the brightness in the eyes and the sweet look on the face. Even the tuft of grass at the angel's knee speaks of his later interest in all facets of nature.

Of the four figures in the painting this one angel is significantly better than the others, the rest being by Verrocchio (John the Baptist), Botticelli, Credi and various other students. It is said that after seeing Leonardo's angel Verrocchio never again wanted to raise a brush, humiliated at how an apprentice could be so much better than his master. It's known Verrocchio gained the least satisfaction from painting and had many other talents to draw on, like sculpture and metalwork.

An x-ray of this painting showed that the original sketching Verrocchio did for Leonardo's angel was entirely different from the final result. This shows that even at this early stage he was freeing himself of his master's coaching to follow his own path. It's interesting to compare the two angels, Leonardo's playing close attention to the action, the figure looking quite natural and part of the activities. In contrast, Verrocchio's angel stares off into space with no interest in what is going on, he looks entirely bored.

The draperies on Leonardo's angel are rather stiff and hard. While learning his art Leonardo would make clay figures which were covered in linen dipped in more clay. This produced a curious system of folds and it is most likely these draperies were painted from drawings made using this process.

In addition to the angel, Leonardo retouched the hair on the second angel and contributed to the background by painting the area directly above the angel's heads. Verrocchio's style was very much traditional for the day; distant plains and hills with the formalized rocks and the occasional scattered tree, often with a somewhat plastic look. Leonardo's work already showed great originality with water, mists, sunlight and shadow.

The angel and Leonardo's part of the landscape are painted in oil; this was a new medium and at the time of this painting it had just been introduced to Italy. Verrocchio's portions of the picture are in the traditional egg tempera which produced a surface similar to enamel but demanded strict demarcation lines between colors. It was very typical of Leonardo to embrace the new medium while his master continued using the old.

Madonna of the Carnation

This painting is a free variant of the Benois Madonna in the Hermitage, being more complex in its composition and spatial arrangement, though perhaps somewhat high-flown and less spontaneous. How it arrived at the Alte Pinakothek in Munich, after its acquisition by a private German collector, is unknown to us. What is certain is that after a comprehensible, temporary attribution to Verrocchio or his shop, art critics subsequently almost universally assigned the painting to Leonardo, a judgment backed up by the most recent research. In fact, the richness of the drapery, the vastness of the mountain scenery with purple and gold hues tingeing the foothills of peaks that fade into the sky, the vitality of the cut flowers in the crystal vase and the softness of the Child's flesh that foreshadows the tender putti of the Virgin of the Rocks, are elements that show a distancing from the more distinctive Verrocchiesque style and instead assume those formal and chromatic characteristics that would be the mature Leonardo's very own.

In the *Madonna with the Carnation*, the skillful foreshortening of the Virgin's hands and the fatty folds of the child's body are a testament to his study of the life model. The chiaroscuro modeling of the figures conveys their three-dimensionality in a way made possible only by the study of light and shade in nature.

The colors of the Virgin's costume are subdued by shadow indicating an unprecedented awareness of the complex effects of light on color. The light that illuminates the forms comes from the upper left and not from the windows. The effect is artificial and yet totally convincing. The folds of the Virgin's veil are reminiscent of Leonardo's studies of water. It spills over her left forearm in a similar manner to the waterfall in Leonardo's *Landscape Drawing*.

The central and centered motif is the young Virgin Mary seated with Baby Jesus on her lap. Depicted in precious clothes and jewellery, with her left hand Mary holds a carnation (interpreted as a healing symbol).

The faces are put into light while all other objects are darker, e.g. the carnation is covered by a shadow. The child is looking up, the mother is looking down — there is no eye contact. The setting of the portrait is a room with two windows on each side of the figures.

Unfortunately, *Madonna with the Carnation* has deteriorated badly and due to an improper restoration the surface has taken on a leathery look; this is especially obvious on the Madonna's face.

Ginevra de' Benci

This oil on wood painting is one of da Vinci's very early works, and is usually dated as c. 1474, a time during which Leonardo was still with Andrea Verrocchio, and had been for about eight years. It was long debated as to whether Leonardo was behind this work; acceptance came with the realization that during the period of 1470-1480 there were no other painters capable of such an impressive painting.

The lady is normally accepted to be Ginevra de' Benci, one of the most gifted intellectuals of her time. Historians generally consider the portrait was commissioned to celebrate the occasion of her marriage on January 15th, 1474 to Luigi Niccolini. She was seventeen; he was thirty four. Marriage portraits were a common practice at the time and most Florentine portraits of women were painted for just this reason.

A number of things support this theory. On the reverse of the portrait is a heraldic motif consisting of a sprig of juniper encircled by a wreath of laurel and palm, along with the motto "Beauty adorns Virtue". The juniper plants are a symbol of chastity, highly appropriate for a marriage portrait, as well as being a pun in Italian on her name. The Italian name for juniper is ginevra.

Unlike Leonardo's other portraits of women, this lady looks sulky, unforgiving and haughty; this is emphasized by the slightly smaller cast of one eye, making her look withdrawn. Her left eye seems to gaze directly at us while the right looks beyond to some invisible point. Like other Florentine women of the period Ginevra has shaved off her eyebrows (this is also obvious in the *Mona Lisa*). Maybe her expression indicates she was not entirely happy regarding her forthcoming marriage. In later life she was to go into self-inflicted exile in an attempt to recover from a severe illness; she was also tormented by an ill-fated love affair.

The marble appearance of her complexion, smoothed with Leonardo's own hand, is framed by the undulating ringlets of her hair. This then contrasts beautifully with the halo of spikes from the juniper bush. Leonardo veiled the background of this portrait in a thin veil of mist known as *sfumato*; this being created with overlaid oil glazes. Though Leonardo did not create this effect he become well-known for his skillful use of it.

At some point this canvas has had as much as on one-third cut from the bottom. This area would have been large enough to show her hands, folded or crossed, and resting in her lap. Their loss is a great shame as no one painted hands as beautifully as Leonardo.

However the loss may not be complete. The silverpoint drawing, to be found in the Royal Library at Windsor, could well be a sketch done in preparation for the Ginevra portrait. Mentally placing these fingers on the painting shows us that the fingers of her right hand would have been touching the laces of her bodice. This area of the portrait has been repainted and in normal circumstances an x-ray might well reveal the missing fingers, if that same area had not been damaged and a new piece added. As a side note, this same hand sketch is thought to have inspired Escher's very famous hand drawing.

Mutilation and repairs aside, this portrait is the best preserved of Leonardo's early works. This was the only privately-owned painting by Leonardo. In 1967 it became the first one of his paintings to join an American museum when the National Gallery in Washington bought it for a record five million dollars.

Benois Madonna

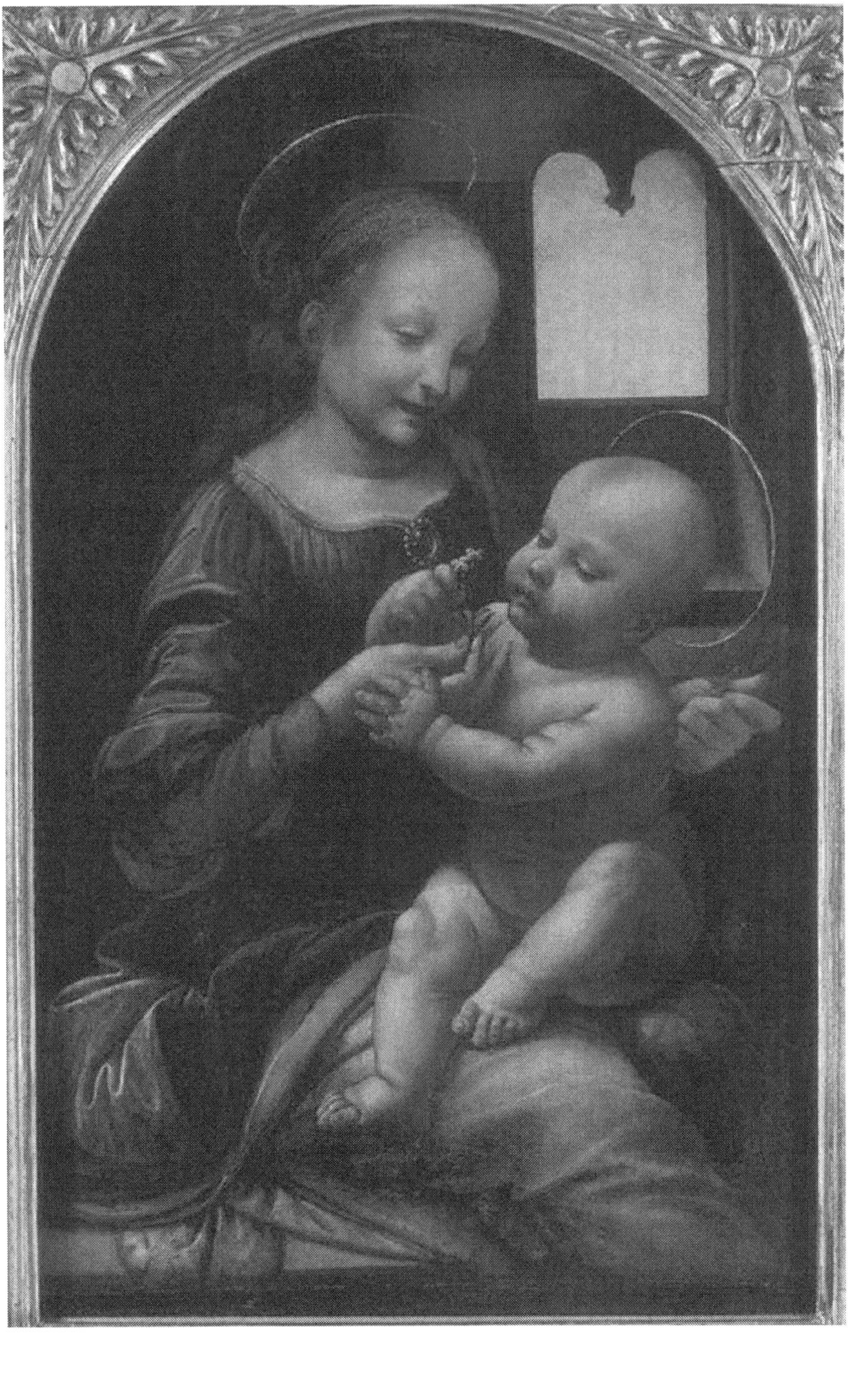

The "Benois Madonna" (1478) is often identified as "Madonna with a Flower." Residing today in the Hermitage Museum in St. Petersburg, Russia, the painting is considered to be one of the earliest done by Leonardo da Vinci (1452-1519), painted when he was just 26.

Unlike many of da Vinci's other works, this shows a playful Madonna, clothed in the Renaissance style of the day (as is her hair style) holding out a flower to her child, Jesus. As a child, the baby holds a cross (the symbol of the Christian church) in his hand, akin to a toy rather than a sacred object.

Although there is some doubt about the attribution to da Vinci, the "Benois Madonna" was likely painted independently by Leonardo when he was studying under the Master Andrea del Verrocchio.

By age 20, Leonardo was considered a Master himself, and a member of the Guild of St. Luke. However, his allegiance to Verrocchio was strong, and they continued to collaborate long after his "official" training was done.

While this is considered one of Leonardo da Vinci's earliest works, he did some preparatory drawings before the painting was completed. One shows the Christ child playing with a cat. This was likely the precursor to the "Benois Madonna." Many of the drawing's characteristics mirror the final painting.

The year 1478 was a critical one for the artist, and his new art would take him to a much grander scale. In addition to making a separation from Verrocchio, he was also making alliances with the Medici family, which would provide him with work via commissions. During the same time frame in which the " Benois Madonna" was being created, da Vinci was commissioned to paint a work for the altar at the Chapel of St. Bernard and "The Adoration of the Magi" for the monks of San Donato a Scopeto.

What sets this painting apart from his larger works is the intimacy captured in the "Benois Madonna." The perspicuity of the Madonna's love for her child is perfectly captured in her expression. There is warmth, freshness, and naturalness in the emotive styling of the mother and child, as well as a playfulness rarely seen in such a religious subject. This could be any mother and child. Only their halos and the baby holding a cross that gives the subject matter away.

The painting technique of the "Benois Madonna" has also been remarked on. The depth of coloring and use of light and shadow set it apart from contemporary works. The painting was also much admired by other artists; for example, Raphael painted his own version in "Madonna of the Pinks" (1506-1507), which depicts another youthful mother handing her son carnations.

Perhaps confusing is the nomenclature of "Benois Madonna." For centuries, "Madonna with a Flower" disappeared. In 1909, however, the painting suddenly appeared in an exhibition of paintings by Architect Leon Benois, who eventually sold it to the Hermitage in 1914.

It seems that the painting had been transported from Italy to Russia in the 1790s, most likely by Art Aficionado Alexander Korsakov. Upon his death, Korsakov's son sold it to a merchant, with the painting eventually making its way into the hands of Benois family in 1880.

The Adoration of the Magi

The *Adoration of the Magi* measures a sizeable nine feet by eight feet. Leonardo was commissioned in 1480 to paint this work for the main altar of the monastery of San Donato a Scopeto, near Florence. He was to complete it within thirty months, but it remained largely unfinished and was left behind in Florence when Leonardo set out for Milan the next year.

The original contract for this painting was particularly complicated with the monks offering Leonardo payment in the form of a third of some land they had received in a bequest. Rules were attached to this in that the property was unable to be sold for the three years following the completion of the painting, except back to the monks and for the price of 300 florins. Along with the land came an outstanding legacy of 150 florins which Leonardo was expected to repay in installments, (this he never did due to lack of money and when the first installment came due he actually requested the monks give him an advance of 28 florins so he could continue work).

He was also asked to provide all paints and gold required for the panel though limited help was given in the form of an advance. Lastly, there was a penalty clause by which Leonardo lost everything if he failed to deliver on time. Leonardo was notoriously unreliable at completing commissioned works. He would devote months to the problems of content and composition but quickly tired of the physical act of carrying out the painting itself.

In *Adoration of the Magi* we have people of all ages surrounding the Virgin and Child, including some on horseback. Leonardo's work was notable for the way he usually attempted to express almost human emotion in his animals. The stairs of a ruined palace can be seen in the background and a procession of people, both mounted and on foot, approaches to join in the worship.

Off to the extreme right and isolated from the rest of the painting stands a shepherd lone boy. It is thought this may be the only ever self-portrait of a young Leonardo and be based on a bronze statue in which he posed for his master Verrocchio. At the time it was common for painters to include themselves somewhere in their works.

Among the other figures we can see an old man, his face twisted on the brink of death, there's a young man lost in thought, the Kings of the East and St. Joseph. Behind the Pagan ruins can be seen a stretch of countryside and mounted men fighting a vicious beast. Ruins such as those in *Adoration of the Magi* were a commonly used symbol to show the decay of paganism after the birth of Christ.

The palm tree shown directly behind the Virgin and Child is the Tree of Life. Sixty-six human beings and eleven animals have been counted in this painting. A highly ambitious project, Leonardo was just twenty-nine when he worked on it.

There are many sketches and experimental drawings in existence which were done in preparation for this painting, in fact more sketches have been found for this artwork than any other piece by Leonardo. People were drawn in a myriad of poses, horses were sketched and re-sketched. Leonardo held a hope that his prancing horses from the *Adoration of the Magi* could be successfully cast in bronze. It seems he never did work out an answer to the problem of how to balance the weight of all that bronze on just the hind legs of the rearing animal.

The perspective study done for *Adoration Of The Magi* is much more 'wild' than the final painting and differs in many areas. It shows a tangle of men and animals across the balcony, the arches and stairs in good condition, naked people crawling up them, a man swings an axe as though trying to chop down one of the columns and amidst the mayhem a camel reclines quietly.

This is the only time a camel appeared in Leonardo's art and it is unknown where he would have seen such an animal; the best guess was the small zoo then at Florence. In any case this animal and all of the other elements listed above were changed or eliminated once painting commenced. In an even earlier sketch for this painting Leonardo drew the figures of the wise men naked so he could then clothe their forms correctly.

Though the *Adoration of the Magi* never progressed beyond its brown ink and yellow ocher groundwork it is recognized as one of his most important works, done at a time when he was taking the final steps away from the influence of his master, Verrocchio. It shows themes which would later appear in much of Leonardo's work, a certain dreamlike quality with an edge of foreboding. When Leonardo departed for Milan Fillippino Lippi was commissioned to complete an alternative painting; this he finished in 1496.

St. Jerome in the Wilderness

This unfinished masterpiece of Leonardo da Vinci depicts an old man with the body of a youth who has a lion laying down in front of him.

Leonardo's treatment of Jerome's years in the wilderness depicts the saint, clean shaven and down on one knee. His traditional attribute, the lion, fills the foreground of the picture. A muscular arm holds a rock in readiness for penance as the saint beats his own breast. The head is similar to Leonardo's anatomical studies of the head and neck of an old man and is quite skeletal in its appearance. Jerome's gaze is drawn towards a crucifix which is sketched on the upper right of the picture. The landscape is typical Leonardo, as is the unfinished figure of the Saint who is portrayed as an ascetic, living his life in the desert or countryside and devoting his life to god.

Jerome spent the last thirty-four years of his life living in a hermit's cell near Bethlehem. His translation of the Old Testament from the original Hebrew is one of his greatest works and resulted in his canonization by the Catholic Church.

At some stage the head was cut out but later rediscovered, the completely restored work was then placed in the Vatican gallery. Also the date of the picture, once thought to be 1481/82, has now been revised as possibly 1488/90 at time when Leonardo was in the service of the court in Milan. The type of wood used for the painting is walnut, a support used by Leonardo after he left Florence for Milan in 1482. All of his work in Florence was painted on poplar wood supporting the Milan date for the work.

Madonna Litta

Though a drawing exists to connect Leonardo with this painting its attribution to Leonardo has been a great source of controversy. There is little doubt he had a hand in the unsigned *Litta Madonna*, but it is awkwardly composed and more than likely was completed by his pupil Boltraffio, around 1480-1490.

The tilt of the Madonna's head is typical of Leonardo and there also exists a drawing of this portion of the painting which is definitely by his hand. However, scholars who have studied the painting point out that the Christ Child bears little resemblance to others Leonardo produced. It is therefore likely that Leonardo designed the pose for this work -- and completed the Virgin's head -- with the rest of the painting being completed by another artist, perhaps Boltraffio, under the supervision of the master.

This work shows the Madonna suckling the Christ Child. Note the lack of halos in this painting; several Madonnas attributed to Leonardo display this same trait.

Litta Madonna passed from the hands of the Vicontis into the Litta family of Milan and takes its name from them. After this it was purchased by a Tsar; then in 1865 by Emperor Alexander II who added it to the Hermitage where it was transferred from wood to canvas. At this point in time it was completely repainted -- for the second time; the first repainting was done by an unknown Milanese artist in 1495.

Replicas of this painting are common, strongly indicating it was a famous composition.

Virgin of the Rocks

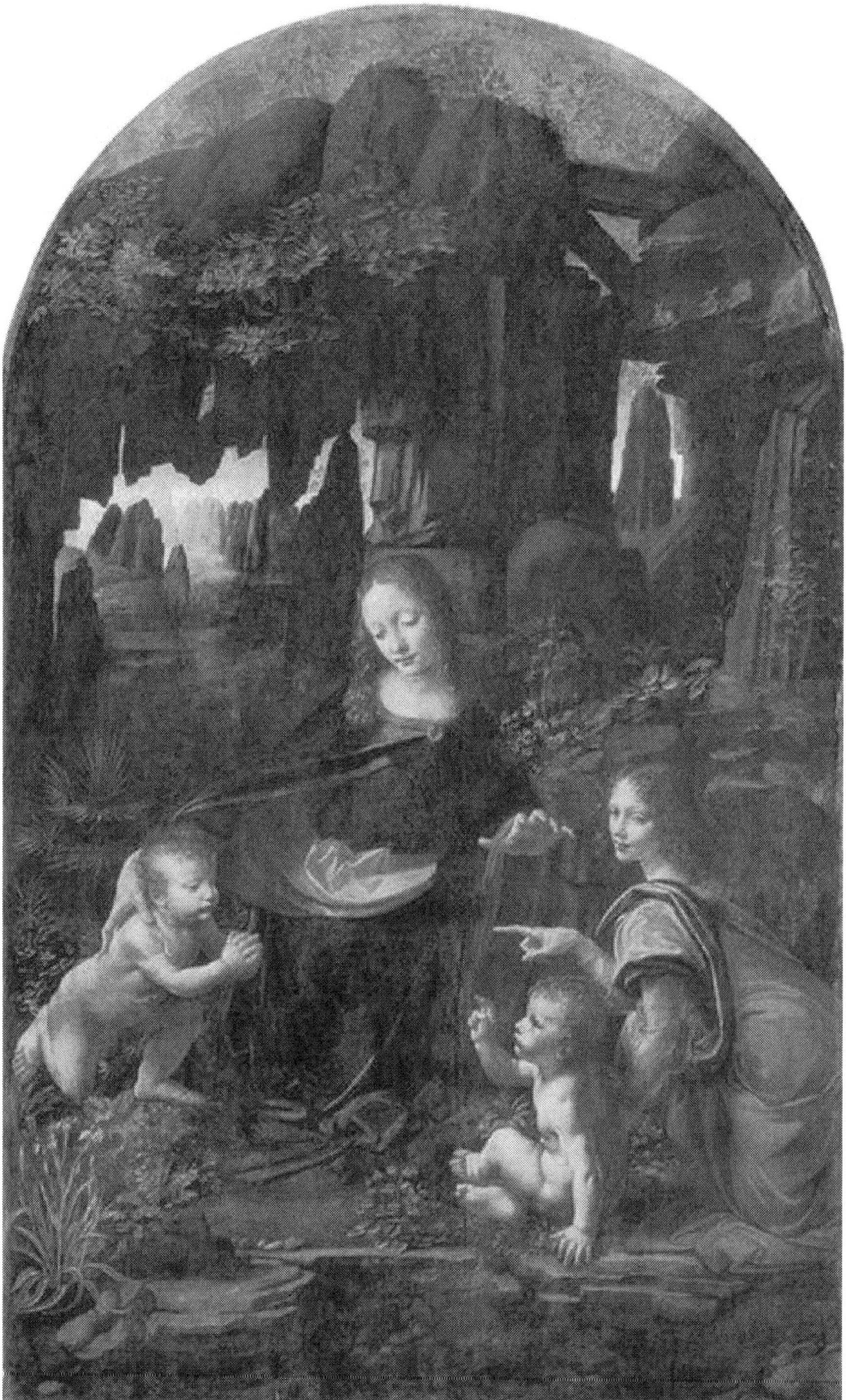

Louvre

On the 25th April 1483, Leonardo was contracted to deliver an altarpiece which would decorate the chapel of the Immacolata at the church of San Francesco Grande in Milan. At the same time Evangelista De Predis was assigned the task of carrying out the gilding, coloring and retouching with his brother Ambrogio to do side panels. Giacomo del Maino was commissioned to carve the framework and once finished the pieces would resemble a miniature temple.

Leonardo's contract had a very short deadline which required the painting be delivered before December 8th, the feast of the Immaculate Conception, (this strongly suggests that the artists already had a cartoon prepared), but as was typical of him he failed to comply; this piece then became the source of two lengthy lawsuits which lasted for the many, many years.

Two versions of this painting exist, one at the Louvre in Paris and the second held by the National Gallery in London. Experts have studied both closely and consider the Louvre version to be entirely by Leonardo, while the National Gallery version is still the source of some debate. The favored suggestion is that de Predis and Leonardo collaborated on this painting after he failed to meet his contractual obligations. Others think Leonardo was less involved in the second version and apart from a few touches, he simply oversaw de Predis. The Louvre painting may have been given by Leonardo to King Louis XII of France in gratitude for settling the law suit between those who commissioned the works and the painters; this would have created the need for a second artwork.

Critics continue to take issue with which is the earlier version of *Virgin of the Rocks* and there is no proof either way. It appears that the style of the Louvre version belongs more to the 1480s and this painting was probably completed early in 1490. The London painting is a more mature work and assuming it is the later version, dates to around 1506.

The contract was very complicated and carefully designed to ensure the monks received precisely the picture they wanted:

Item, Our Lady is the centre: her mantle shall be of gold brocade and ultramarine blue. Item, her skirt shall be of gold brocade over crimson, in oil, varnished with a fine lacquer...Item, God the Father: his gown shall be of gold brocade and ultramarine blue. Item, the angels shall be gilded and their pleated skirts outlined in oil, in the Greek manner. Item, the mountains and rocks shall be worked in oil, in a colorful manner.

Some changes were made to this description, St. John was introduced while an angel was removed. The side panels required four angels on each, singing and playing harps. Documents recently found show Leonardo's painting was eventually set in place on 18th August 1508, with the final payment for it being made in October of the same year.

The *Virgin* or *Madonna of the Rocks* is the first work that Leonardo executed in Milan. It addresses the theme of the Immaculate Conception; this being the belief that the Christ child was conceived without original sin on Mary's part. This was a hotly debated topic in Leonardo's day and he was required to convey the purity radiating from the Virgin. In both paintings she was depicted as flat-chested and sitting in a cavern surrounded by phallic rocks and womb images. The setting was perfect for the chapel as it was built over catacombs.

The paintings illustrate a popular story of the time. It is that of Jesus meeting an infant John the Baptist, who is in the care of the angel Uriel. Both are on the run to evade Herod's massacre of innocents. As John pays homage to Jesus he is blessed and the Baptism prophesied; this explains the pool in the foreground of the Louvre version.

The plants in Leonardo's works are interesting as they were painted directly from nature during a time when most artists simply copied from the books of herbalists. Leonardo would carefully choose plants for their symbolic value. In the Louvre version of the *Virgin of the Rocks, Aquilega*, or columbine (dove plants) are beside the Virgin's face; these symbolise the Holy Spirit. Stains on the St. John's wort suggest a martyr's blood, the creeper *Cymbalaria* symbolises constancy and virtue. Heart-shaped leaves represent love and virtue; sword-shaped leaves, the sword of sorrow which was to pierce Mary's heart and the palm leaves are a symbol of victory.

The Louvre version, considered to be wholly by Leonardo, is set in the autumn. The original sketches showed the angel as very feminine; this was changed in the final painting where the angel can be seen as either male or female. It was first mentioned as being in the royal collection at Fontainebleau in 1625.

Virgin of the Rocks in London's National Gallery displays a number of changes from the Louvre piece. It brings the viewer closer to the figures, is much bluer and has an air of flowing waters. Other new or changed elements include St. John's cross of reeds; the hand of the angel which no longer points at St. John; the halos and the lighter drapery. Both the halos and the cross were a later addition done by an unknown artist.

Portions of the painting are slightly unfinished, the left-hand of the angel being one area. It is also likely that the foreground was intended to be contain a pool similar to that of the Louvre version. The 'plastic' look of this painting almost immediately led scholars to consider it a collaboration. Areas to compare are the rocks which seem badly lit, and the flesh of the children which is flat looking.

This version remained in the chapel until 1781; it was then taken to the hospital of Santa Caterina in Milan. Collectors went to great lengths to obtain Leonardo's works, no matter how small. In 1875 this panel was purchased by the Scottish painter, Gavin Hamilton, who took it from Italy to London, then sold it to the Marquis of Landsdown. It passed into the hands of the Earl of Suffolk, finally entering the National Gallery in 1880. The two side panels of the de Predis brothers joined it in 1898; these depict the musician angels. All three paintings are now displayed together and appear as they would have in the chapel.

The dispute over fees and the legal battles with the monks is thought to have been regarding the London copy only. Leonardo and Ambrogio -- Evangelista having died in 1490 -- had sent an appeal for extra funding, pointing out that not only had the project required in the contract been completed, but that the frame alone had absorbed almost all of the entire eight hundred lire fee which had initially been agreed on.

In terms of payment they had actually only received one hundred of the twelve hundred lire that were asking. As a result they requested that the "oil painting of Our Lady" be withdrawn, so they could consider selling tit to other interested buyers. This request was refused and in 1503 Ambrogio tried once again, this time petitioning Louis XII of France, but Leonardo was no longer in Milan and the case was deferred.

Things were finally settled on 27th April, 1506. It was determined that the work was, in fact, unfinished with the result that Leonardo was not paid for the first painting, it then being forfeited to the artist. He agreed to do a second work -- or to have another artist do one on his behalf -- and to deliver it on time. The deadline was be two years and for this he would receive half of the additional payment he had asked for the first painting, the sum of two hundred lire.

The subject of the Immaculate Conception was a popular one of the day and was taken up again and again by pupils of the Leonardo school.

The identification of the child figures may be confusing to the modern viewer in part because they are not accompanied by obvious iconographic clues revealing their identifies. The figure on the left is St. John, and the figure seated on the right is Christ. Adding to this confusion is the fact that not only is the Christ Child not seated in the Virgin's lap, but she is not even touching her son. Instead, her hand is on the back of St. John, who knees in adoration toward his cousin. Christ, in turn, blesses St. John.

The gestures and glances among the figures results in a more dynamic portrayal of the Virgin and Child that seen in earlier Renaissance paintings. Whereas a painting such as Masaccio's Holy Trinity showed figures which related to one another to a limited degree, Leonardo has created a scene in which all the figures interact through gestures and glances to create a more unified whole.

 The angel on the right glances out at the viewer while pointing at St. John, whose gaze toward Christ provides a main focal point of the painting. The Virgin also gazes down at her son, and the placement of her left hand reinforces the emphasis on Christ. The connection between the Virgin and St. John is then made by the placement of her right hand. Thus, although the pyramidal composition is something that had been employed by Renaissance artists for decades, the way Leonardo made all the figures interact in a naturally-engaging way is different.

In addition to the dynamism of the figural group, the *Virgin of the Rocks* is also noteworthy for its rocky, almost mysterious setting in which the figures are placed. It is not the type of heavenly space symbolized by the golden background of older altarpieces, such as those by Cimabue, Giotto, or Duccio. Nor is it an idealistic landscape that can be found in Fra Filippo Lippi's painting of the Virgin and Child. Instead, it is dark, misty, and cavernous.

On the left side in the distance, the forms become less distinct as they get lost in a haze of foggy atmosphere, which illustrates the implementation of aerial perspective. The very smooth transition between colors and between light and dark that Leonardo used in this painting is called *sfumato*, which means "smoky". Not only is it visible in the landscape, but also in the figures, who are cast in light which smoothly turns into areas of dark shade. It is similar to the traditional *chiaroscuro* technique used by earlier Italian painters, but it is more refined and elevated to convey a higher level of visual realism.

London

Portrait of a Musician

Much debate surrounds this painting dating from the same period as *Lady With The Ermine* (c. 1482-1483). If indeed Leonardo was the painter, *Portrait Of A Musician* would be the only portrait he did of a man. This painting is completely lacking in documentation and there is no record of anyone ever having commissioned it. Often considered to be his least important work, the fates have arranged that it should be the best preserved.

The first issue that arises with this panel is who really painted it. While hanging in the Louvre (1796-1815) it was listed as being by Bernadino Luini. In Milan, before and after that time, it was usually attributed to Leonardo. Other experts consider the artist was either Giovanni Antonio Boltraffio or Ambrogio de Predis.

The second issue is that of who the sitter was. In the nineteenth century the catalogue of the Biblioteca Ambrosiana listed this painting as "Portrait of Ludovico il Moro"; that was accepted without question until a 1905 cleaning revealed the sheet music along with the letters 'CANT...ANG...'. Now there was no doubt the subject was a musician, but which one was a another matter. Was it:

Franchino Gaffario, choirmaster of Milan cathedral, (the text could be an abbreviation of the words *Canticum Angelicum*).Attalante Miglioretti, resident in Milan until 1490.Angelo Testagrossa, singer and singing master (perhaps the inscription reads *cantor Angelo?*)

Most historians think the portrait is probably of Franchino Gaffario but the connection is tenuous at best, as is evidence that this painting is by Leonardo. Various historians, remembering Leonardo's fondness for puzzles, have tried to read something into this piece of sheet music, so far without luck.

So, what makes this panel a possible Leonardo da Vinci? The answer lies in a certain kind of portraiture and common characteristics which exist in each of his portraiture works. These include the following things:

- Backgrounds left in shadow.
- Figures shown at half-length or slightly more.
- Subjects carefully positioned at a three-quarter turn so as to improve viewer identification of the sitter.

Despite the third point, Leonardo's subjects remain largely unidentified. When it comes down to the nitty gritty all we can say for certain regarding *Portrait Of A Musician* is what we see in front of our eyes; things like how well the artist obviously understood the bone structure beneath the flesh, how unforced the pose is, the exquisitely curling hair and elegant fingers very common to Leonardo's work. Leonardo himself was a very fine musician.

Heavily restored and repainted this work was left unfinished, though at quite an advanced stage. The face and hair are well worked and the notes of a musical partition can be clearly seen. The remaining elements were left in the state of an advanced draft, this is most obvious in the tunic worn by the subject.

Lady with an Ermine

The painting, *Lady With The Ermine*, is thought to date from Leonardo's early years in Milan (c. 1482-1483). Like all of his portraits (with the exception of the *Mona Lisa*), there is some disagreement about this painting. Some historians consider that the sitter is Cecilia Gallerani, mistress of Ludovico Sforza (the Duke of Milan). Renaissance women contrived to look middle-aged before they were twenty and if it is her she would only have been about seventeen at the time. Another suggestion is that the painting is from a little later, around 1491, and that the woman is Ludovico's wife, Beatrice d'Este.

The third theory is that the subject may have been La Belle Ferronniere, a nickname given to the mistress of Francis I of France. Though some support for this idea came from an inscription in the upper left-hand corner which reads LA BELE FERONIERE LEONARD DA WINCI, most experts now consider this to be incorrect. The inscription is not original, but is a later addition.

Speculation also exists over whether this painting is partially or entirely by Leonardo, or possibly by Ambrogio da Predis or Boltraffio.

Lady with The Ermine has been heavily over painted. The entire background was darkened, her dress below the ermine was retouched and a transparent veil being worn by the woman was repainted to match the color of her hair. The result of this last retouching has been to give the appearance that her hair reaches down and underneath her chin. Yet another change was the addition of dark shadows between the fingers of her right hand, a close look at the bottom two fingers shows they are quite inferior to the others after an unknown restorer repainted them. An x-ray of this painting revealed the presence of a door in the original background.

There are a number of things to support the idea this is Cecilia Gallerani, and that it was painted by Leonardo himself. Firstly, the ermine was used as a heraldic figure by Ludovico, it appeared on his coat of arms. Secondly, despite the heavy retouching of the painting the woman's face and the animal are intact, and the colors used were those Leonardo favored during his first years in Milan. Despite her young age at the time of this portrait, Cecilia had already been seduced by Lodovico, had borne him a son and held a very commanding position at court.

The strongest pointer of all is a request made in 1498 from Isabella d'Este. She asked for the portrait on loan as she wished to see a sample of Leonardo's work. Cecilia replied on the 29th April saying she would have sent it with even greater pleasure if it had been more like her. She begged the Marchioness not to think this was the fault of 'the master', explaining it was done when she was very young and since that time she had changed so much no one would recognize it as being her. This also helps to date the picture. To help further in the dating we have a sonnet by the Court poet, which was written about the portrait. In this, he said that she 'seemed to listen and not to speak'. A study of the apparent mood of the subject shows this to be an apt description. Poet, Bernardo Bellincioni, died in 1492 so the portrait must be prior to that date.

Leonardo composed his paintings using geometric proportions, and mathematical principles discovered by the ancient Greeks; this was typical of Renaissance painters. In this painting the pyramid is the invisible base upon which he built. Particularly interesting about the design of this painting is the lack of straight lines. It is composed almost entirely of curves which carry the eye from the woman's head, down to the right, across the ermine and then back up the other sleeve. The only almost straight lines to be seen are the band on her head and the square-cut neckline on her dress.

The delicate little animal has been identified as an ermine in its winter coat; according to legend these animals died if their white coats became dirty. These animals were considered to be a symbol of chastity from as early as the third century after Christ; its use here is somewhat ironic considering that in this period a woman was required to be chaste, but also a most devoted mistress.

The presence of the ermine also injects a subtle touch of humor to the portrait since its Greek name of galee offered a pun on her own name. Leonardo reproduced an amazingly wide variety of animals in his work and said of the ermine that it "does not eat other than once a day, and it will rather be taken by hunters than escape into a dirty lair."

In Leonardo's time apprentices would make soft-hair brushes with bunches of fur from the tail tips of ermine or stoats. Brushes were made by fitting the fur to a small piece of quill; this, in turn, had a wooden handle attached to it. Harder brushes were made of white pig's bristles. Prior to use on a fine painting these would be softened by use whitewashing walls. The ermine is related to the Russian sable, an animal whose fur is used for the manufacture of very high-quality modern brushes.

La belle ferronnière

Cecilia Gallerani was Ludovico Sforza's first mistress and Leonardo painted her in the form of *Lady with the Ermine.* Later, the Duke was to take another mistress, Lucrezia Crivelli, and she is thought to be the subject of this painting. An alternative suggestion, though less accepted, is that this painting is Isabella of Aragon.

This may, or may not be, Leonardo's work. The pose is stiff, which would be unusual for Leonardo, and the woman's features are thicker and heavier than those normally found in his portraits. Bernard Berenson once said of this portrait, "one would regret to have to accept this as Leonardo's own work." Those in favor of this being a genuine Leonardo point to the knotted ribbons on her shoulders and the cords around her neck which do resemble Leonardo's style.

It may be that this work was done by an apprentice, or Leonardo may have been forced to do some traditional Milanese courtly portraiture at the whim of his patron; tradition demanded an unnatural pose as shown in this painting. It also placed great importance on showy dresses, jewellery and other decorations, as shown in this work. Another possible answer is that this was a joint project carried out by several artists at the School of Leonardo, and based on a design by him.

Done around 1495 this painting takes its name from the *ferroniere* the sitter wears around her brow, a common Lombard fashion. In the nineteenth century this work was much admired and widely copied, though no other artist managed to capture the beautiful modeling of the face. It is thought the painting may have originally been balanced with an architectural element on the left but this is one work over which there are more questions than answers.

Sala delle Asse

Leonardo was responsible for the decoration of the ceiling and vault of the *Sala delle Asse* (translation: 'room of the tower' or 'room of the wooden boards') in Sforza's castle, Milan and although this cannot be considered a 'painting' in the usual sense of the word to not mention it would be unforgivable. He was presented with this room for his own use; access being gained via a bridge and arcade he had built over the moat.

Painted between 1495--1497, the fresco is made up of eighteen willow trees, two of which skillfully encircle two windows in the room . Where the boughs meet towards the ceiling they intertwine, thought to be a symbol of the marriage of Ludovico, Duke of Milan with Beatrice d'Este.

Emblazoned throughout the branches is a fantastic golden rope made up of assorted loops and knots. Appearing to be several ropes, if it is followed the viewer discovers it is actually just the one cord which folds back on itself, twisting and turning throughout the entire pattern. Gold rope was a fashionable symbol of the day and appeared knotted on the clothing of Beatrice d'Este. Included in the work is the coat of arms of the Sforza family (falcons and serpents) which is painted in the very centre of the ceiling where the tree branches meet. Finally, four tablets were hung in the corners of the room to record important historic and political events of the day.

Much of the work on the 2,880 square foot canopy was carried out by Leonardo's pupils, but he did the design and this is a play on the word *vinci*, one meaning of which is willow. The search for any other hidden significance among the designs still continues, however it appears there is none to be found.

The hall was then used as a barracks and the paint deteriorated and flaked away. In 1901 a restoration was begun by Luci Beltrami; just enough of the original paint remained for this to be successful, but the work done was so extensive that the fresco was largely remade and repainted. Beltrami completed the restoration by taking the few remaining traces of the original and repeating the designs and motifs until the entire vault was covered. Like the *Last Supper*, this is not the work Leonardo would have originally presented to the world.

Further restoration went on in 1954 during which time a thorough cleaning of one small area was done and some boards removed which had been left untouched during the previous restoration; this revealed to some extent exactly how much the fresco had been altered by over painting. Originally the work was more open between the trees and branches, with the paint being less heavy, the leaves and branches more wavy. Large rocks were revealed through which roots were intertwined rising into huge tree trunks. Restorers of 1954 restrained themselves from completely removing all of the reconstruction done by Beltrami, restricting their own work to removing the heaviness evident in the new painting. With this they hoped the scene would achieve a more naturalistic look something Leonardo would have aimed for.

The Virgin and Child with St Anne and St John the Baptist

Leonardo first explored the topic of the *Virgin and Child with Saint Anne* around about 1498. His original sketch is now lost to us, but in the one illustrated below, commonly termed the *Burlington House Cartoon*, the infant Christ is shown blessing a young St. John during a meeting in the desert. This is only one of many sketches on the theme that was never translated into a painting; Leonardo was to entirely abandon these earlier ideas.

Cartoons are preparatory large-scale drawings intended to be transferred to a wall or canvas during the final painting; this one was named after the British collection which once owned it. Many scholars prefer the *Burlington House Cartoon* to Leonardo's completed oil painting, pointing out how the face of the Madonna is much more natural and less wooden looking.

The *Burlington House* cartoon covers eight sheets of tinted paper and is drawn in charcoal with chalk highlights. It is one of the most important works in the National Gallery, London who keep it in a darkened room to prevent fading.

When originally exhibited in Florence this cartoon received an acclaim almost comparable to that of a completed painting and it has long been considered one of Leonardo's finest works, easily on a par with the *Last Supper*. Though Leonardo never painted this cartoon it inspired another artist to produce the *Virgin and St. Anne* .

The oil painting of the *Virgin And Child With St. Anne* is thought to date from 1507-1513. We owe this panel to the modesty of Filippino Lippi who turned down the commission and suggested Leonardo as, "a greater artist".

An account of the cartoon for this painting indicates it may have been modified at some stage, perhaps as an afterthought. A description of the original sketch describes St. Anne as restraining her daughter from discouraging the Child in pulling the lamb's ears. This is not what can be seen today; our view is of a rather detached watching grandmother. It is quite possible the original concept for this painting had St. Anne's hand lying on her daughter's sleeve; this could easily be cancelled out by painting the Virgin's sleeve over the top of it.

In the painting the infant is shown holding a lamb, this is symbolic of himself, as Jesus is often termed the 'lamb of God'. The angle of the lamb's head, and the tight woolly curls repeated on the head of the Child, connect the two. Continuing the idea of connections, Leonardo has positioned the two sets of arms like links in a chain. Atop the chain is St. Anne, slightly set apart in the composition by the line of the Virgin's shoulder, her downward glance and the use of darker skin tones on her face. Behind them the trees definitely belong to the earth while the mountains and lake seem almost heavenly. Though this work has been much acclaimed, it has also been much criticized due to the very artificial poses.

The five by four foot painting was commissioned by the monks of the Santissima Annunziata in Florence for their high altar. Some consider this painting to be a treasure of esoterica and occult wonders. Some are fascinated by the sight of St. Anne supporting her heavy daughter on her knee, and with no visible means of support. Others are convinced that hidden in the folds of the draping over the arms is the shape of a vulture, the head and neck can be found in the blue cloak encircling the Madonna and the bird's tail points towards the infant's mouth. Most are skeptical about this idea, though Dr. Sigmund Freud supported it and claimed that it was a repercussion of a fantasy Leonardo had when he was a child and which he noted in *Codex Atlanticus:*

"Among the first recollections of my childhood it seemed to me that, as I lay in my cradle, a kite came to me and opened my mouth with its tail and struck me several times with its tail between my lips. "

Freud saw this as a "passive homosexual fantasy" and thought it also accounted for the strange and bewitching smiles on the lips of many of Leonardo's subjects.

The *Virgin And Child With St. Anne* has been retouched, and was left unfinished with the drapery covering the Virgin's legs being little more than an outline. Why is unknown, though it may have been due to Leonardo's increasing interest in mathematics and subsequent engagement as engineer in the service of Cesare Borgia. In places the paint has been applied so thinly it is almost transparent allowing the underlying sketch to be visible. The appearance of this worsened after a 1953 cleaning of the oil on wood artwork, during which over painting was removed and dark varnish lightened.

A close study shows the lamb has been completed by another artist so the painting may have been abandoned at a time when the lamb had still only been sketched in. The background, St Anne, the Virgin and the Child are thought to be from the hand of Leonardo himself though some doubt exists about the heads as they lack the fine texture of the Mona Lisa. Suggestions have been made that these were worked on by a pupil of Leonardo's.

At the same time this painting was in progress Leonardo was experimenting with preparations which he hoped would result in an improved varnish for his work; unfortunately these experiments were a failure. This mattered little; Leonardo still had 10 years to live, but by 1508 his career as a painter was drawing to a close and after maybe as much as ten years of intermittent work on this painting he gave up.

With Leonardo not completing *Virgin and Child with St. Anne* in time for the altar, Filippino Lippi decided to return to the task, working on a *Deposition*. He was to die before having the chance to finish his painting and it was finally completed later by Perugino.

Portrait of Isabella d'Este

Leonardo da Vinci left Milan in 1499 when the French army invaded Italy. On his way to Venice he stopped at Mantua, where Isabella d'Este asked him to paint her portrait. This famous drawing is a sketch for the portrait that was never painted; despite its fragile state of conservation, it is one of Leonardo's finest head-and-shoulders portraits, here with the head in profile. It is also the only known drawing by the master that is highlighted with several colored pigments.

Isabella d'Este wanted to have the best possible portrait of herself painted, sculpted, or struck on a coin. In 1498, she determined to surround herself with the most eminent contemporary artists and find the best portrait painter, one who could produce a perfect imitation of nature; her choice fell on Leonardo da Vinci. When in Venice, Leonardo da Vinci showed his portrait of Isabella to his friend Lorenzo da Pavia, who wrote to the Marchesa on March 13, 1500: "Leonardo da Vinci is in Venice, he has shown me a portrait of Your Ladyship that is very lifelike. It is very well done and could not possibly be better." Despite Isabella's insistence, the painting was never done.

In his sketch, Leonardo used various pigments (sanguine and chalk), different tones of black, and finely hatched and smudged red and yellow ochre to obtain the passage from light to shadow on the face and hair. Contrary to claims by Vallardi and almost all subsequent authors, there are no traces of pastel. A very pale white applied to the bosom (covered by a piece of lace called a "modesty piece"), the forehead, and the cheek, accentuates the slant of the shoulders and the shadow of the neck.

Though unfinished, this sketch is remarkable for its proportions, and for the foreshortening of the bust; it is also striking for the ambiguous choice of pose. The perfectly linear profile, eyes gazing beyond our field of vision, contrasts with the turn of the body. The portrait in profile may have been the choice of the Marchesa herself, who was thus portrayed on the bronze medal made by Gian Cristoforo Romano in 1497-1498.

The clear-cut profile of the face, its use of space, the slant of the turning shoulders, the attention paid to the folded hands and the finger pointing to the book are all touches that distinguish this work from the Portrait of Cecilia Gallerani (1489-1491, Cracow, Czartoryski Museum) and from the Portrait of an Unknown Woman (c. 1495-1500, Paris, Musée du Louvre). This portrait of Isabella d'Este can be seen as the fruition of Leonardo's experimentation since the 1490s, and a preview of what was about to follow: the cartoon of the Virgin and St Anne (London, National Gallery), and the Mona Lisa (Paris, Musée du Louvre). The portraits of Isabella d'Este and the Mona Lisa seem to represent Leonardo's "progressive idealization of the portrait"—in other words, his attempt to create portraits that were lifelike yet of a perfection related to universal beauty.

The Madonna of the Yarnwinder

When Leonardo returned to Florence from Milan in 1500, he is known to have started work on a painting for

Florimond Robert, secretary to King Louis XII I of France, the so-called Madonna of the Yarnwinder. The painting is described by the Carmelite monk Puetro da Novella in a letter dated 14 April 1501, to Isabella d'Este, Marchioness of Mantua. Isabella had been trying to persuade Leonardo (without success) to produce a painting based on a cartoon of her likeness done by Leonardo the previous year. Novella describes the yarnwinder painting in some detail.

The little picture he is doing is of a Madonna seated as if she were about to spin a yarn. The child has placed his foot on the basket of yarns and has grasped the yarn-winder and gazes attentively at the four spokes that are in the form of a cross. As if desirous of the cross he smiles and holds it firm, and is unwilling to yield it to his Mother who seems to want to take it away from him.

At this stage in his life da Vinci seems more preoccupied with his scientific studies rather that any attempts to complete paintings, this is highlighted in Novella's a previous letter to Isabella.

"He has done nothing else save for the fact that two of his apprentices are making copies and he puts his hand to one of them from time to time. He is hard at work on geometry and has no time for the brush".

Several versions of the painting exist, among these two are considered to be of such quality that they can be attributed, at least in part, to Leonardo himself. These are the Buccleuch Madonna and the Lansdowne Madonna.

One of the most interesting and complete sketches Leonardo ever did was for this painting; a close look shows this work was based around the geometric figures of triangles and ellipses. An excellent red chalk drawing of the Madonna's head and shoulders also exists in the Royal Collection at Windsor Castle.

This work, intended for Florimond Robertet, Secretary to the King of France, shows the winder as shaped like a cross; this symbolizes the Passion of Christ and His future death. It appears that Mary wants to pull the Child away from the symbol of His future, but even she is powerless to prevent the Crucifixion which is part of His destiny. Of the two works one is very green whilst the other is quite blue; the landscapes also differ significantly with one showing a vicious mountain range beneath a vivid blue sky while the other runs down to the sea.

Leonardo prepared for paintings that included the Christ child or the infant St. John the Baptist by drawing dozens of studies of little children. Most of his children appear between nine and eighteen months, all are shown nude and all look similar enough as to make the viewer wonder whether the one child modeled for each painting.

This painting is sometimes called *Madonna of the Spindle* or the *Madonna with the Distaff.*

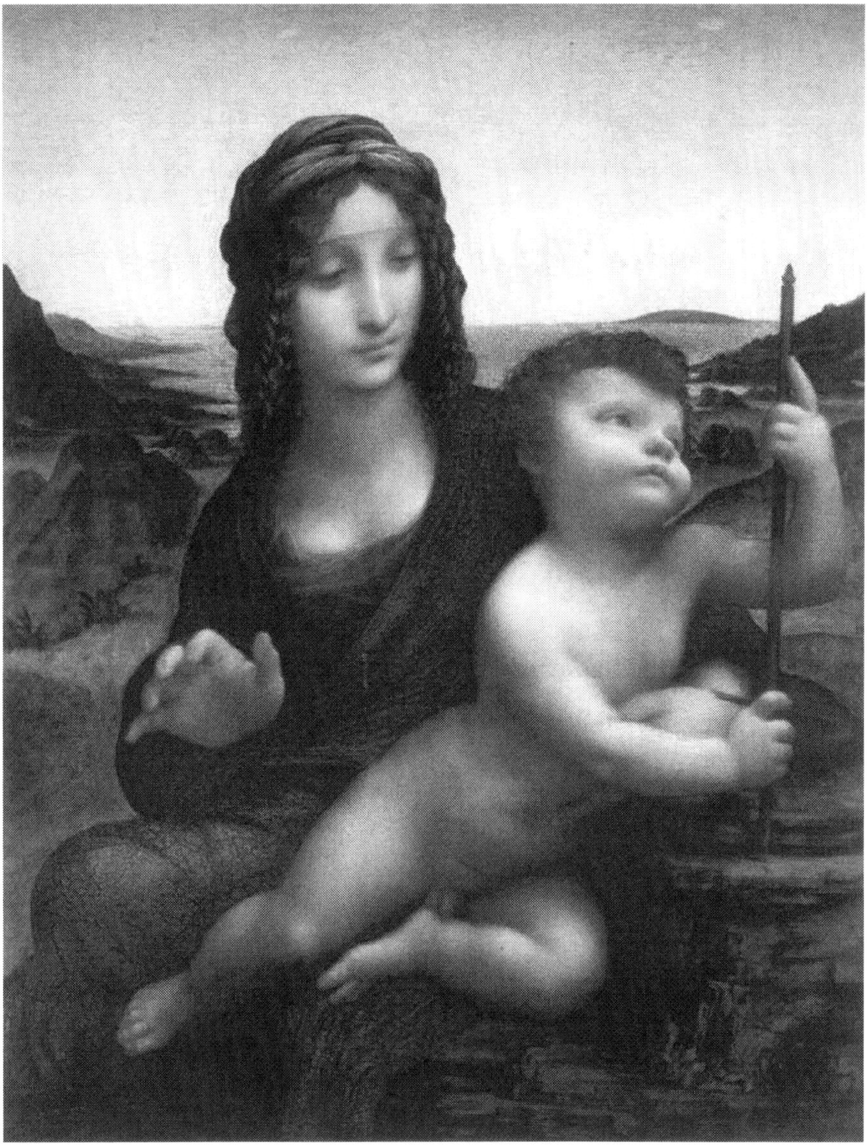

Bacchus

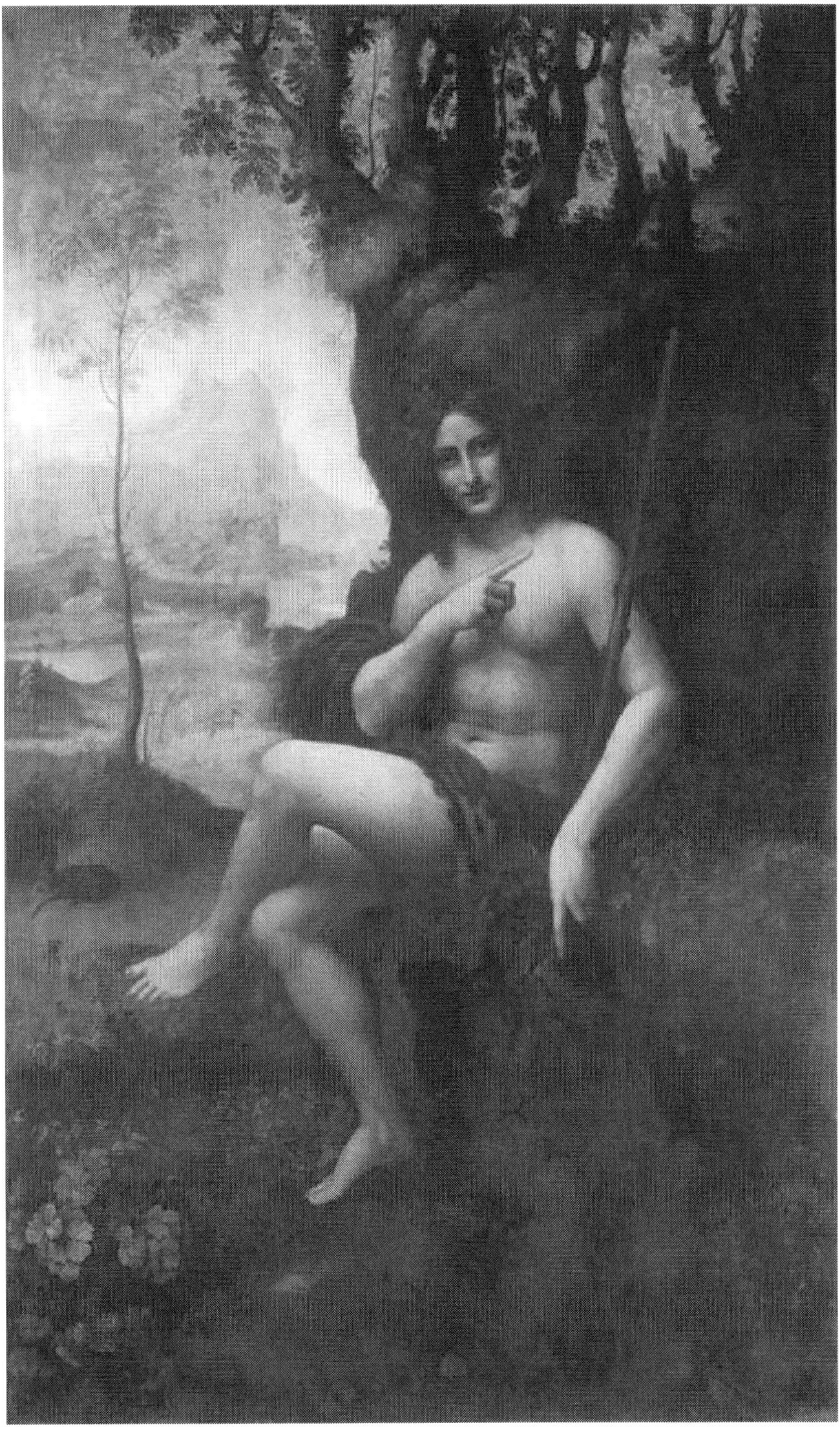

The Louvre holds this artwork of *Bacchus* which some have ascribed to Leonardo. Transferred to canvas at some stage during the nineteenth century others consider it was more likely to have been painted by Cesare da Sesto, Bernazzano, Francesco Melzi or a 'Lombard painter'.

Deterioration of this painting has made it difficult to judge who the painter may have been, but the background does not seem to be typical of Leonardo, lacking his descriptive qualities. On top of this no preliminary studies have been found for this artwork. However, the pointing finger in this painting indicates that whoever the painter really was, the original subject is likely to have been St. John and the painting was originally called *St. John the Baptist in the Desert,* a name which was later changed to *Bacchus in a Landscape.*

A number of items were later additions: the panther skin, crown of vine leaves and grapes not being part of the original work. The cross in the crook of St. John's arm also had the bar removed changing it to a thyrsus.

The male figure in the painting looks a lot like Salai, the male lover of Leonardo.

Salvator Mundi

It is believed that seventy-five percent of Leonardo's works have been lost to us so therefore any new discovery causes great excitement and serves to alter our view of his art. An excellent example of this is *Salvator Mundi*, (literal meaning: 'Saviour of the World'), which is now considered to be authentic.

Louis XII started negotiating with Leonardo in 1506 and the painting was finished, as much as it would ever be, by 1513. It was delivered after the Queen's death and so Louis decided he would donate it to the religious order connected with her in Nantes. A century later Queen Henrietta Maria of England saw the painting and had an etching made of it by Hollar, to add to a series of famous paintings he was doing for her. In the nineteenth century the convent was dissolved and the painting sold on to Baron de Lareinty of Paris; he had it until 1902 when it was again sold, this time to Comtesse de Béhague. It has remained in the family having been passed onto his nephew and then to his son, Jean Louis de Ganay.

Various tests and close examination has convinced experts this painting is genuine. Monochromatic sodium lighting, infra-red and ultra-violet tests were performed and, along with x-rays, these have revealed a number of interesting details:

- The pearls around the jewel have been altered.

- A cross has been removed from the orb (not very successfully).

- Leonardo deviated from his basic sketch very little. Infra-red tests showed up the original sketch behind the painting.

- X-rays show the paint has been applied in layers on a wooden base. This technique was used often by Leonardo during his last five years of work.

- A thick coat of varnish has been added.

Nut wood was used for *Salvator Mundi*, the same as used on *St. John the Baptist*. The triangular composition, light angles, facial shadows and hair swirls are typical of many of Leonardo's paintings, while the colors used are reminiscent of the *Last Supper*.

Typical of Leonardo, many of the objects in this painting have a deeper significance which is not at first obvious to the eye:

The eight-pointed centre star signifies resurrection and corresponds to the eight lines of the threads found on the stole. The ruby represents martyrdom and passion. An unusual vestment tuck seen on the right-hand side of the stole signifies the lance piercing Christ's side. What we now see as a globe was originally an orb (when surmounted by the cross); it probably recalls the words, "I am the Light of the world."The stole symbolizes the Voice of Immortality. Catholic priests don stoles as a sign of accepting the New Covenant.

Vasari, known for his wonderful description of the *Mona Lisa* even though he had not laid eyes on it, also described Salvator Mundi:

"In his head, whoever wished to see how closely art could imitate nature, was able to comprehend it with ease, for in it were counterfeited all the minuteness's that with subtlety are able to be painted. Seeing that the eyes had that luster and watery sheen which are always seen in life, and around them were all those rosy and pearly tints, as well as the lashes, which cannot be represented without the greatest subtlety. The eyebrows, through his having shown the manner in which the hairs spring from the flesh, here more close and here more scanty, and curve according to the pores of the skin, could not be more natural. The nose, with its beautiful nostrils, rosy and tender, appeared to be alive. The mouth, with its opening, and with its ends united by the red of the lips to the flesh-tints of the face, seemed in truth, to be not colors but flesh. In the pit of the throat, if one gazed upon it intently, could be seen the beating of the pulse. And, indeed, it may be said that it was painted in such a manner as to make every valiant craftsman, be he who he may, tremble and lose heart."

Vasari also described this work without laying eyes on it too.

Self-portrait of Leonardo da Vinci

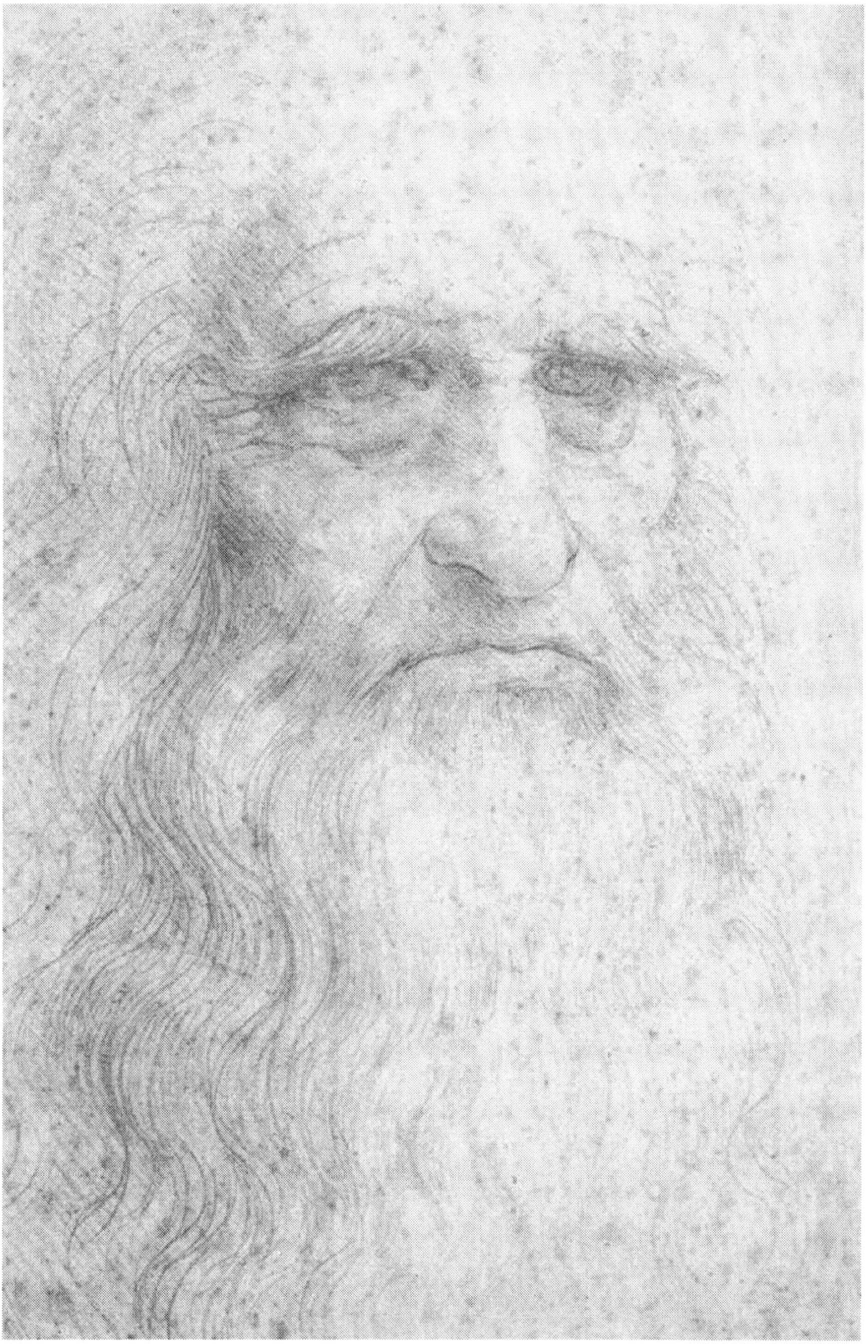

Dated circa 1512 and done with red chalk on 33.3 cm × 21.6 cm paper, Leonardo da Vinci's self-portrait illustrates the three quarter view of an elderly man's head. The depicted man was shown with long and wavy hair and beard flowing down to the man's shoulders and chest. Deep lines were made on the facial features of the man especially in the part of the eyebrows and the lines below the eyes forming pouches. The eyes were illustrated looking somewhere ahead. The fine lines and shadings were ingeniously done.

This self-portrait illustrates da Vinci as a man of wisdom since the long hair and beard are not common during the Renaissance era. There are other self-portraits of da Vinci and some of them were in some of his paintings, such as in the Adoration of the Magi where one of the figure surrounding Mary and the child Jesus was allegedly a self-portrait of the young Leonardo da Vinci. The drawing resides in Turin, Italy in the Royal Library where public viewing of the artwork is not allowed due to the drawing's poor condition.

The Battle of Anghiari

The fresco of the *Battle of Anghiari* was to have been painted in the Council Hall in Florence and stand opposite the *Battle of Cascina* by Michelangelo. These were events the Florentine Republic saw as worthy of commemoration, Anghiari being a victory over Niccolo Piccinino, the mercenary commander of Milan, and Cascina a victory over Pisa. When finished they would flank the throne of the Gonfaloniere, the chief executive. The up-and-coming Michelangelo (twenty-seven at the time), and the established master, Leonardo, were developing a strong rivalry at this time. They had formed a severe dislike for each other and Leonardo seemed to consider painting alongside Michelangelo as a personal challenge. Michelangelo, for his part, called Leonardo, "the lyre-player from Milan." This was destined to be the battle of the Titans, with a third young artist popping in sometimes to view the progress. The artist was Raphael, who was about 21 at the time.

An ambitious painting, Leonardo used a type of plaster which he read about in a book by Pliny, with the unfortunate result that the work he had barely begun was irreparably ruined. Problems started as soon as Leonardo placed his brush to the wall at 9 am. The weather turned bad, the sky opened and it rained then on until nightfall. The sudden humidity liquefied the paste holding the cartoon in position; as Leonardo lifted his hand to start work the cartoon slid to the floor and tore.

An encaustic (translation: 'fixing by heat') technique was that chosen for the artwork. Leonardo took the precaution of doing a trial run of this technique; it was applied to a board and dried well in a warm environment. Firstly a layer of granular plaster was applied, this being primed to a hard flat finish; over this was added a layer of resinous pitch which was applied with sponges. The combination should have supplied a suitable base for the application of oils. During the painting process an ingenious scaffolding was used to raise Leonardo to the needed height for finishing the upper portion of the centre section of this work, but though the scaffolding was a brilliant design, the painting methods chosen were absolutely disastrous.

Because of the techniques used the colors refused to dry naturally. In an effort to overcome this a large fire was lit beneath the wall to apply a heat treatment. The upper areas then dried far too hard, while the colors from lower down simply ran and merged; at this point Leonardo gave up. There have been many suggestions as to why this project failed so spectacularly. The master may have been trying to outstrip his younger rival and hurried the process, or the resistance to drying may have been caused either by faulty linseed oil or defective plaster which rejected the colors. What is certain is that Leonardo failed to note an important part of Pliny's instructions which said:

"Those among the colors which require a dry, cretaceous, coating, and refuse to adhere to a wet surface, are purpurissum, indicum, caeruleum, milinum, orpiment, appianum, ceruse. Wax, too, is stained with all these coloring substances, for encaustic painting; a process which does not admit of being applied to walls...."

Over the next few years what little remained of the painting crumbled so all we have left is eight composition studies, three large studies of heads, a written description, and inaccurate copies done by various artists.

Around 1603 Rubens' produced a copy of Leonardo's *Battle of Anghiari*. Based on an engraving done by Lorenzo Zacchia in 1558, its design has many variations on the original, including the heads of all of the combatants, their weapon styles and their armor or drapery. Yet Reubens achieved something in this painting that no other artist has managed to portray, that is Leonardo's sense of power, confused fury and intense violence. Reuben's *Battle of the Standard* is sometimes incorrectly portrayed in books, or on the Web, as being the original painting by Leonardo, which it most definitely is not.

One other often overlooked copy of *Battle of Anghiari* is of interest. This is a drawing done by Rucellai and copied directly from the mural painting itself. Being contemporary with the original work it has great importance because it is as close to an accurate copy as we will ever see. When this drawing was done some parts of Leonardo's mural were unfinished, this can clearly be seen in the sketch where the artist remained faithful to the original work by also leaving his drawing incomplete.

Unfortunately Rucellai was not familiar with Leonardo's presentation, so he translated the wall painting in his own style, losing the fiery, intense display from the master. Reubens later recaptured that style, but sacrificed the accuracy.

Judging from what remains, the central theme from Leonardo was that of a melee of horses and men interlaced with flames and smoke. In three episodes, the first section showed two fighting men mounted on horseback. The second hexagonal segment gave to this work an alternative title of *Battle of the Standard* and featured the intense struggle for the colors. Finally we had the cavalry pictured as held in reserve.

This was much less than agreed to under the terms of Leonardo's contract which demanded that -- starting from the left -- Niccolo was to be shown issuing strong commands to his men; the Milanese approach in a cloud of dust; St. Peter would then appear to the Patriarch leader of the papal troops who would go to the rescue; the fight for the River Tiber bridge; the arrival of the Patriarch's forces to back up the Florentines; the enemy retreating; the dead buried; the trophy erected. Together these would depict the beginning, middle and end of the battle.

Even with an area of 54 ft by 21 ft Leonardo was forced to simplify these demands greatly. The two soldiers to the left are Milanese and it is probable that the one with the upraised sword is Piccinino, the Florentines are then shown charging but St. Peter doesn't put in an appearance anywhere. In the distance is a town with tents which provides the backdrop for fighting soldiers. The section of painting Leonardo did complete shows horses fighting each other with barred teeth, they display terror and aggression.

Commissioned in 1503, Leonardo's agreement promised he would complete the work by February 1505 or return all payments. Despite his non-completion and no indication he was making further significant progress, the payments continued after time ran out. The end result was a terse letter regarding his work which was sent from Pier Soderini to Charles d'Amboise. It stated that "Da Vinci has not behaved toward the Republic as he should have, because he accepted a large sum of money and has scarcely begun the great work he was to execute." Leonardo later arranged to leave anyway. It is interesting to note that although there were other pictures commissioned from various artists to mark the Republic's development, none was ever finished. This includes the one by Michelangelo who started work on a full-scale cartoon in 1504 and was then called away to Rome by Pope Julius II. All that remains of his work are copies of the cartoon which showed soldiers being surprised while bathing nude in the Arno.

Due to his use of experimental techniques, Leonardo's completed centre section had vanished almost entirely within only fourteen years. Vasari then painted a chaotic battle scene over the area. Ultrasonic tests were carried out in 1976; they searched for traces of Leonardo's painting and none were found.

Leda and the Swan

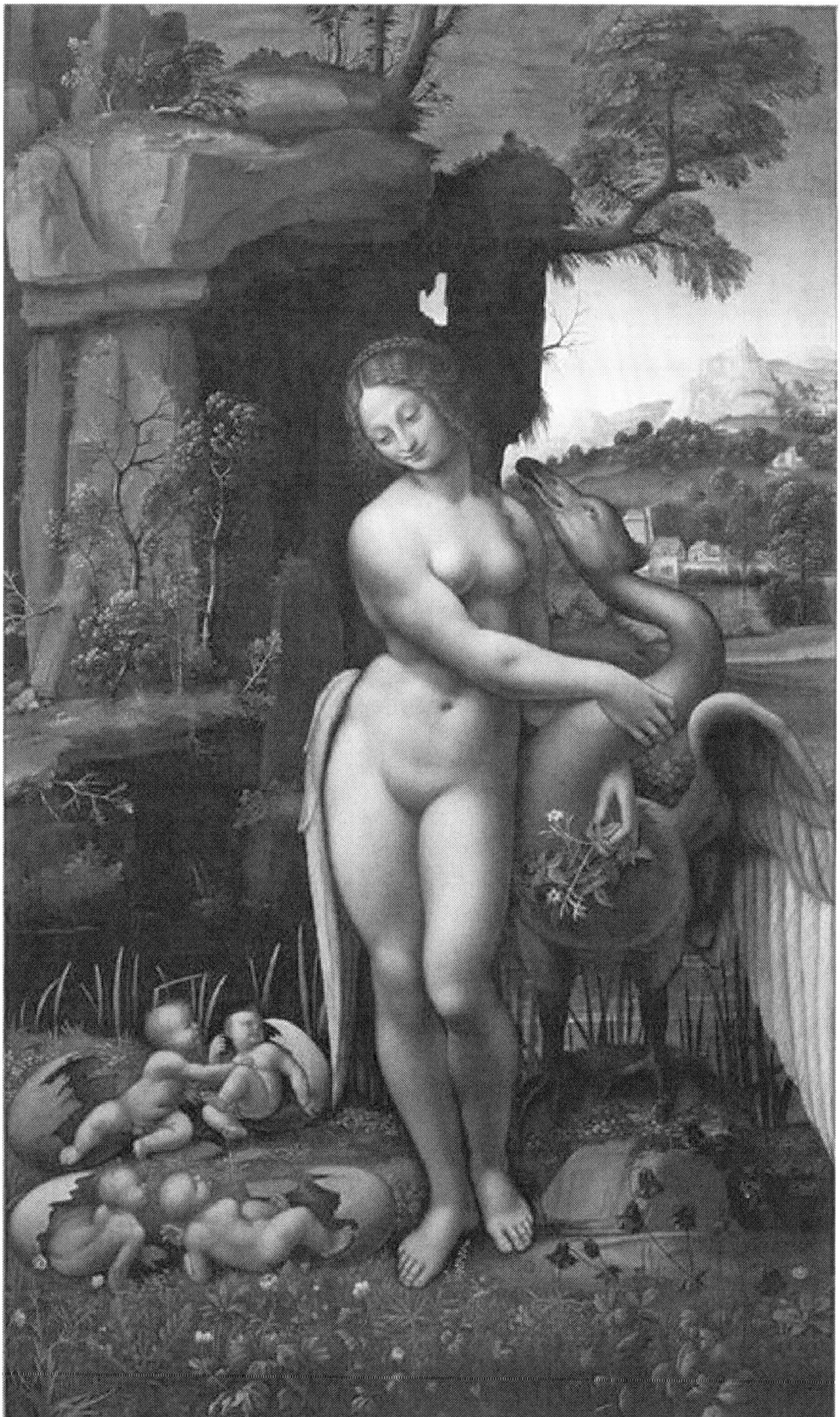

Melzi version

Leonardo was very absorbed with the theme of Leda during the time he was working on Mona Lisa and while in Milan he made many sketches of the swans in the moat around the Castello. The picture was described by Cassiano del Pozzo in 1625; at this stage it was in the royal collection in Fontainebleau:

"A standing figure of Leda almost entirely naked, with the swan at her and two eggs, from whose broken shells come forth four babies, This work, although somewhat dry in style, is exquisitely finished, especially in the woman's breast; and for the rest of the landscape and the plant life are rendered with the greatest diligence. Unfortunately the picture is in a bad state because it is done on three long panels which have split apart and broken off a certain amount of paint."

By the eighteenth century the artwork was completely lost to us; fortunately several things remain to give a good idea what it looked like. There are Leonardo's drawings of the head and bust of Leda; a famous drawing done in 1506 by Raphael; a red chalk drawing which may have been done by an assistant to Leonardo; a picture by Bugiardini which was based upon Leonardo's original cartoon (done in 1504); another copy probably by Francesco Melzi and based on Leonardo's second cartoon (drawn around 1508); plus a copy by another pupil, Cesare da Sesto; this final work is said to be closest to Leonardo's original and is displayed in this book. Leonardo's head and coiffure study for *Leda and the Swan* is signed; it should be noted that this is not his signature, having been added at a later date by one of the owners.

Of the two cartoons Leonardo did for this work one showed Leda kneeling and used mostly curved lines to suggest a writhing movement which emphasized fertility; the other had her in a standing position. In the final painting Leda was in the second of the two poses and seeming to recoil from the swan, while at the same time showing a shy attraction towards it. Leda's head was modestly lowered giving a virginal look, in contrast her figure was opulent, a mature body with a young head on her shoulders. Like many of Leonardo's subjects her hair was painted in minute detail. She was surrounded by the most fertile landscape that Leonardo -- by this time aged 54 -- had produced since his workshop days. The swan was Jupiter in one of his many disguises and the babies were Castor and Pollux, and Helen and Clytemnestra.

St. John the Baptist

When Leonardo died his possessions were pitifully few. He had three of his paintings, the *Mona Lisa*, the *Virgin and St. Anne* and his final painting, that of *St. John the*

Baptist. This painting dates from his final years in Rome, around 1509-1516.

Many people are critical of this work, finding it a disturbing representation of a character normally portrayed as gaunt and fiery, living in a desert and surviving on a diet of locusts and honey. In Leonardo's painting St. John seems almost to be a hermaphrodite. He has a womanish arm bent across his breast, his finger raised towards heaven, and that same enigmatic smile so admired on the face of *Mona Lisa,* a smile which can be seen in other Leonardo paintings like that of *St. Anne*. His face is almost faun-like and framed by a glorious cascade of curls. The finger pointed towards heaven was to appear quite often in Leonardo's work (the *Burlington House* cartoon is another example) and denotes the coming of Christ.

From the encircling darkness emerges this mysterious figure holding a reed cross and wearing an animal skin. An examination of this painting using monochromatic sodium light has revealed both of these items were added later by a different artist. Two suggestions have been made for the lack of a background:

- It may have been an attempt to focus on the spiritual side of the topic and the presentation was designed to emphasize the saint's isolation.

- Possibly it is the work of another artist and behind the dark shadows there exists a hidden landscape. However, to date no examinations have been able to find concrete evidence to support this suggestion.

Other versions of *St. John* have also been attributed to Leonardo with the Municipal Museum at Basle having one. Also, in a private collection there is a sketch in which *Bacchus* is depicted in a state of sexual arousal. His right hand is upraised with the pointing finger, the angle of the head and facial expression very similar to that of *St. John the Baptist*.

Many of Leonardo's pupils were to copy *St. John the Baptist* and their work appears in various collections. Other paintings mentioned in this article which are on a similar theme and presently thought to be the work of Leonardo may later prove to be those of other artists. Typical of Leonardo's paintings, these will be heavily debated especially as so many copies of his original were done by students.

Also we know how Salai, Leonardo's pupil and lover looks, by the portraits and by the describing of Vasari of him: "a graceful and beautiful youth with fine curly hair, in which Leonardo greatly delighted." .

This painting of St. John the Baptist, Bacchus and Bacchus with an erection in his notebooks all look almost exactly like each other. We can say that Leonardo had Salai model for these paintings.

Vitruvian Man

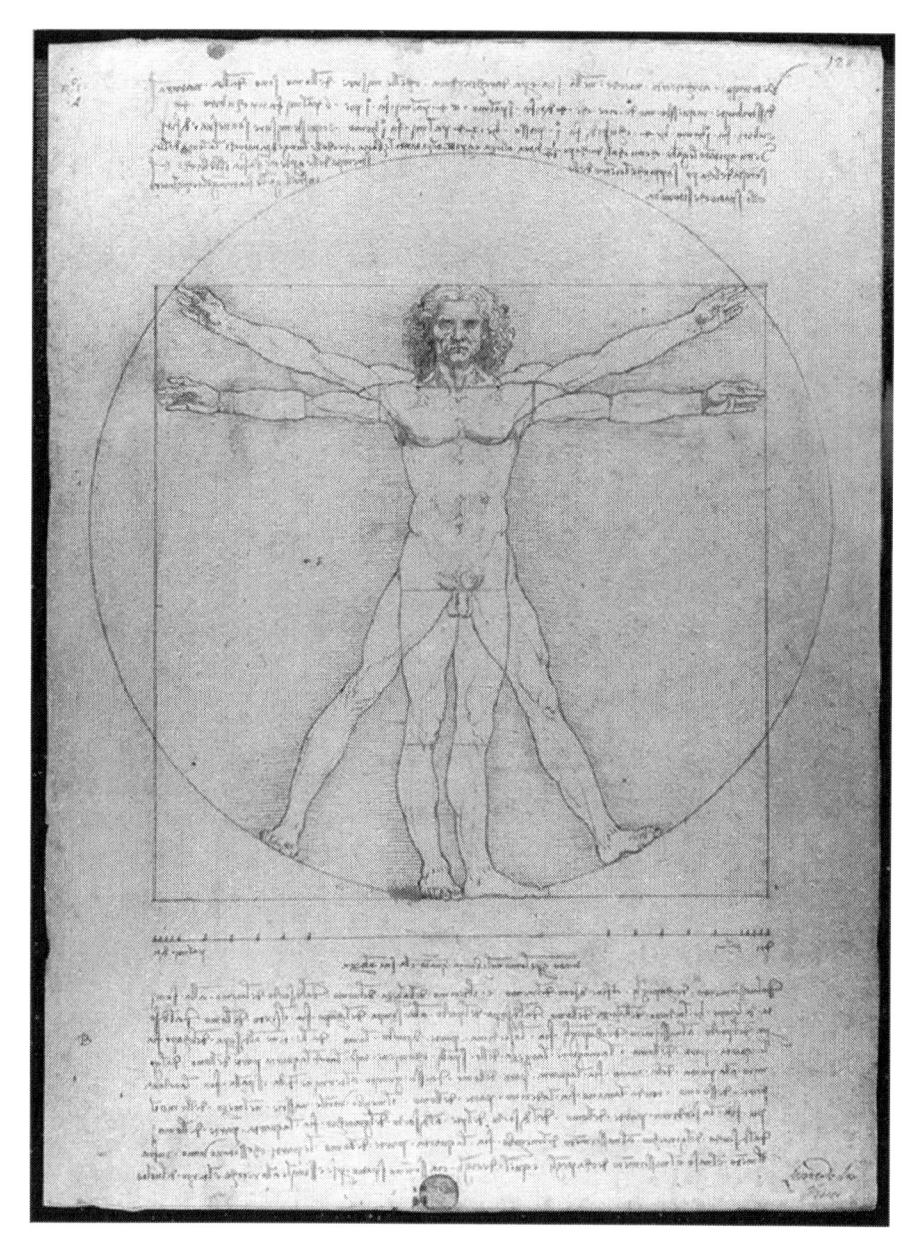

"Le proporzioni del corpo umano secondo Vitruvio" The proportions of the human body according to Vitruvius, is a drawing by Leonardo around 1490. The notes based on the work of architect Vitruvius accompany the art. The drawing was made with pn and ink on paper. It depicts a man in two superimposed positions with his arms and legs apart and inscribed in a circle and square.

The blend of art and science during the Renaissance is demonstrated by this image. It also provides the perfect example of Leonardo's deep understanding of proportion. Leonardo da Vinci believed the workings of the human body to be an analogy for the workings of the universe.

The accompanying text is written in mirror writing. Leonardo used this method to conceal information from his rivals occasionally. According to the text, the drawing was made as a study of the proportions of the male human body as described in Vitruvius. The text is divided into two parts: above and below of the image.

The first paragraph of the upper part reports Vitruvius: "Vetruvio, architect, puts in his work on architecture that the measurements of man are in nature distributed in this manner, that is:

- a palm is four fingers
- a foot is four palms
- a cubit is six palms

- four cubits make a man

- a pace is four cubits

- a man is 24 palms

and these measurements are in his buildings". The second paragraph reads: "if you open your legs enough that your head is lowered by one-fourteenth of your height and raise your hands enough that your extended fingers touch the line of the top of your head, know that the centre of the extended limbs will be the navel, and the space between the legs will be an equilateral triangle".

The text below the painting gives these proportions:

- the length of the outspread arms is equal to the height of a man

- from the hairline to the bottom of the chin is one-tenth of the height of a man

- from below the chin to the top of the head is one-eighth of the height of a man

- from above the chest to the top of the head is one-sixth of the height of a man

- from above the chest to the hairline is one-seventh of the height of a man.

- the maximum width of the shoulders is a quarter of the height of a man.
- from the breasts to the top of the head is a quarter of the height of a man.
- the distance from the elbow to the tip of the hand is a quarter of the height of a man.
- the distance from the elbow to the armpit is one-eighth of the height of a man.
- the length of the hand is one-tenth of the height of a man.
- the root of the penis is at half the height of a man.
- the foot is one-seventh of the height of a man.
- from below the foot to below the knee is a quarter of the height of a man.
- from below the knee to the root of the penis is a quarter of the height of a man.
- the distances from below the chin to the nose and the eyebrows and the hairline are equal to the ears and to one-third of the face.

The points determining these proportions are marked with lines on the drawing. Below the drawing itself is a single line equal to a side of the square and divided into four cubits, of which the outer two are divided into six palms each, two of which have the mirror-text annotation "palmi"; the outermost two palms are divided into four fingers each, and are each annotated "diti".

Leonardo combined a careful reading of the ancient text with his own careful observation of actual human bodies in this drawing. He correctly observes that the square cannot have the same centre as the circle in the drawing. The center of the circle is also the navel of the human. The navel, is somewhat lower in anatomy. This is what makes the Leonardo's painting innovative and distinguishes it from earlier illustrations. Another point he departed from Vitruvius is by drawing the arms raised to a position in which the fingertips are level with the top of the head, rather than Vitruvius' much lower angle, in which the arms form lines passing through the navel.

Since Leonardo took the human body as an analogy of the workings of the universe he made the drawing so the drawing itself is often used as an implied symbol of the essential symmetry of the human body, and by extension, of the universe as a whole.

By studying the drawing, once can realize that the combination of arm and leg positions actually creates sixteen different poses. The pose with the arms straight out and the feet together is seen to be inscribed in the superimposed square. On the other hand, the "spread-eagle" pose is seen to be inscribed in the superimposed circle.

According to recently found evidences, it is a strong possibility that Leonardo have been influenced by the work of Giacomo Andrea de Ferrara, a Renaissance architect and both an expert on Vitruvius and a close friend of his. However, Giacomo Andrea's original drawing has only one set of arms and legs while Leonardo's has the position of his man's arms and legs change.

The Last Supper

The Duke Lodovico chose the church of Santa Maria delle Grazie as his family chapel and burial place. He then commissioned Leonardo to paint the *Last Supper* on the north wall of the refectory, a job which came at the perfect time as Leonardo was experiencing one of his periods of depression. As a rule the topic of the Last Supper was depicted in murals of vast proportions, this mural measures 30 feet by 14 feet, so the work was a challenge from the very start. After three years of sketches, studies and preparatory drawings, only a handful of which remain today, the work was finally completed in 1498.

The work focuses on the scene at the moment of the announcement of Judas' betrayal. In his initial drawings Leonardo followed the tradition of seating Judas opposite

Christ and separated from the other characters, but he later changed this and seated all of the Apostles in groups of three on the same side of the table. He then drew the table as too short and narrow for the thirteen characters to sit around it comfortably and made Christ and the Apostles oversized so they were larger than life. Finally, to focus the eye on Christ, he placed three windows in the background with the largest directly behind His head, almost like a halo. Christ is shown as perfectly calm while the Apostles are in an obvious state of shock.

In painting the *Last Supper,* Leonardo created the effect that the room in which Christ and the apostles are seen was an extension of the refectory. This is quite appropriate, since the Last Supper takes up the basic theme (eating) of the purpose of the refectory.

The scene shows us figures in a rectangular room with coffers on the ceiling and tapestries on either side of the room. The room terminates at three windows on end of wall and through the windows we can see into a beautiful landscape setting. We see how the landscape in the background terminates in a kind of misty, grayish horizon. This painterly device, in which the horizon's colors become more dull and colorless, is called *aerial perspective* and was used by Renaissance artists to create the illusion of depth in landscape scenes.

As far as the composition is concerned, Christ is in center among the apostles, and his body forms a triangle-like shape which is not overlapped by any apostles. There are four sets of three apostles at the table beside Christ, and these numbers may have been important for Leonardo for symbolic reasons (for example, there are four Gospels in the Bible, and three is the number of the Trinity). We can easily see Leonardo's use of one-point linear perspective, in which the vanishing point is at Christ's head (the orthogonals can be seen by following the tops of the wall tapestries or the coffers to where they intersect at Christ), which his also framed by the pediment above and back-lit by the open window behind.

Leonardo experienced his greatest problems with the heads of the Redeemer and Judas. He took the heads of the characters from people he saw around him, but never found models that were sufficiently expressive for the two principal figures. There have been suggestions that Judas was finally based on Savonarola, a dominant figure in Florence. Leonardo's models did not volunteer, nor did they know they had been selected for study. Christ's face was the last to be painted; there exists a pastel study for the head of Redeemer in the Brera Picture Gallery which has been attributed to Leonardo.

Leonardo was often observed at work and people found cause to comment upon his work. Some days he would climb the ladder (the work is not at floor level and was carefully designed to become a natural extension of the room), raise his brush and work all day never stopping, not even for food or drink. Then three or four days might go by without him even being seen. When he finally put in an appearance he could stare at the wall for several hours, suddenly seize his brush, make two strokes and leave again.

The story goes that at one point the prior complained about Leonardo's laziness. When called to the Duke to explain, Leonardo asked, "Do friars know how to paint?" At the time he was searching for the perfect head for the character of Judas and for over a year he had been spending several hours each day haunting ghettos looking for a face which showed the necessary wickedness. His final response to the complaint was to state that the prior had the perfect face and if he was unable to find a suitable alternative he would base Judas on the prior! "Until now I held off holding him up to ridicule in his own monastery."

Judas' hand hovers over a dish ("He that dippeth his hand with me into the dish, he shall betray me.") The character is also distinguished by the angle of his body which shows him as drawing back from Christ whereas the other Apostles all lean forward. Among all of the figures seated at the table the face of Judas is the only one in shadow.

Above the masterpiece are the crests of Ludovico, Duke of Milan, Beatrice d'Este, and their two sons, the Counts of Pavia and Bari. Leonardo's success at painting this work won him back the Duke's patronage and he acquired a vineyard and a piece of property of '16 rods' near San Vittore.

This masterpiece became immediately famous and immensely popular with the public. It is said the French King so loved this work he asked to have the entire wall sawn off and taken to France! This idea was shelved due to the sheer difficulty involved.

Last Supper is now only a pale shadow of the brilliant work it must have been upon completion. Vasari and a number of other historians attributed the painting's poor state of preservation to the chromatic pigments used by Leonardo and indeed they were unsuited to wall painting (the work is oil and tempera). However, more recent examinations and restorations have shown the deterioration is largely due to the humidity which always impregnates the wall and the refectory. *Last Supper* began to show signs of deterioration soon after it was completed and by 1586 it could hardly be deciphered. Numerous attempts at recovery were made, these in no way helped the situation and some even worsened things. In 1652, after serious deterioration had set in, a door was cut through the centre of the wall. The effects of this are still clearly visible across the bottom of the painted tablecloth and at Christ's place; His feet were cut off in the process.

In 1796, the refectory was used as a stable by French troops. Napoleon gave strict orders that no damage was to be done but the Apostles were pelted with clay. Later still the room was used for storing hay and, as if the fates had decided to finish the work off, in 1800 a flood covered the entire painting with green mould.

1943, and the monastery was hit by Allied bombs, blowing the ceiling off the refectory and destroying most of the apse of Saint Maria. Despite having been protected by sandbags it is a miracle that *Last Supper* survived this attack at all. But what little remained of the repaintings and original colours suffered severe damage. Italy's Ministry of Fine Arts decided to make a final attempt to prevent the paint and plaster from turning to dust.

In an attempt to effect repairs master restorer Mauro Pellicioli strengthened the fresco with waxless shellac while also removing all of the repainting. The work was so delicate that frequently restorers were spending the entire day concentrating on an area the size of a postage stamp. The heads of Bartholomew and Philip, the body of Judas and the hands of Christ were all brightened and successfully salvaged; it was also revealed that Christ's robes were once flame red, symbolising the Passion. Small flakes of the original paint were painstakingly attached with a special treatment. The job was completed in 1954, an almost perfect restoration with a tiny area left so people could see what *Last Supper* was like prior to work.

Still, this is not the work Leonardo produced. Very little of the original paint remains and there is nothing to tell us the facial expressions of the Apostles, these had been erased although the outlines of the Apostles were still discernible. At this stage there is nothing more that skill or science can do for the grievously damaged *Last Supper*, it is as close to original and as secure as possible.

Mona Lisa

Leonardo's three great portraits of women all have a strange air of wistfulness. This is at its most engaging in *Lady with the Ermine*, brooding in the *Female Portrait* of Ginevra de' Benci and undeniably enigmatic in the *Mona Lisa*. Unarguably the most famous painting in history, it is also the only portrait by Leonardo whose authorship remains unquestioned. Though neither signed nor dated it is universally accepted to be by Leonardo. But who was the subject, when was it painted and what is the story behind the mystical smile?

Historians agree that Leonardo commenced the painting of *Mona Lisa* in 1503, working on it for approximately four years and keeping it himself for some years after. Supposedly this was because *Mona Lisa* was Leonardo's favorite painting and he was loathe to part with it, however it may also have been because the painting was unfinished. Whatever the reason, much later it was sold to the King of France for four thousand gold crowns. The world has talked about it ever since. After the revolution in France the painting was transferred to the Louvre. Napoleon took possession of it using the panel to decorate his bedroom. Upon his banishment from France *Mona Lisa* once more returned to the care of the Louvre. What is certain is that the painting was never passed onto the rightful owner, that being the man who originally commissioned and presumably paid for it. .

The first written reference to the painting appears in the diary of Antonio de' Beatis who visited Leonardo on the 10th October 1517. He was shown three paintings by the master, who was aged sixty-five at the time. These three consisted of one of the Madonna and Child in the lap of St. Anne, one of a young St. John the Baptist and a third of a Florentine lady.

Who was the lady in question? At this time researchers remain uncertain of the sitter's identity with some claiming she was Isabella of Aragon -- the widowed Duchess of Milan; they point out the 'widows veil' on her head as supporting evidence. Others conclude she was the mistress of Giuliano de' Medici, but the veil on her head may well be a symbol of chastity, commonly shown at the time in portraits of married women. The path shown may also be the 'path of virtue', a reference to the story 'Hercules choice'; this was frequently referred to in Renaissance art and would be unlikely to appear in a painting of a mistress. It is probable that she was Mona Lisa Gherardini, the third wife of wealthy silk merchant Francesco di Bartolommeo di Zanobi del Giocondo. At this stage Lisa would have been over twenty-four years of age, by the standards of the time she was not in any way considered particularly beautiful, though Leonardo saw certain qualities which have now made her the most heavily insured woman in history.

The smile has become a hallmark of Leonardo's style. It is most obvious in the painting of the *Mona Lisa,* but also to be seen in most of his other works. There is no mistaking the same smile -- and upturn of the left side of the mouth -- on the face of St. Anne in the *Burlington House Cartoon.* That drawing dates from a bit earlier than the *Mona Lisa,* somewhere around 1498. Speculation exists that the smile originated from his mother, Caterina. A less romantic suggestion is that the painter merely "concerned himself with certain arrangements of lines and volumes, with new and curious schemes of blues and greens."

Various other suggestions have also been made as to the reason behind the smile including the simple idea that during this period in history women were instructed to smile only with one side of their mouths so as to add an air of mystery and elegance. An Italian doctor's answer was that the woman suffered from bruxism; this is an unconscious habit of grinding the teeth during sleep or times of great stress. The long months of sitting for the portrait could well have triggered an attack of teeth grinding. Leonardo did attempt to keep his subject relaxed and entertained with the use of music; he had six musicians to play for her plus and installed a musical fountain invented by himself. Different, beautiful works were read out loud and a white Persian cat and a greyhound bitch were there for playing with.

The most unusual suggestion is that *Mona Lisa* was really a man in disguise, perhaps being a form of self-portrait and the face of Leonardo himself. Computer tests show some of the facial features match well that of another(?)self-portrait of Leonardo. Some copies of the *Mona Lisa* also show the sitter as a male. Some experts also argue that the sitter is actually Salai himself.

The truth is that this style of smile was not invented by Leonardo da Vinci. It can be found in a number of sculptures from the fifteenth century, one of these being Antonio Rossellino's *Virgin;* it is somewhat reminiscent of Greek funerary statues and Gothic statues in medieval cathedrals. The mysterious smile can also be found widely in the works of Leonardo's master, Verrocchio and Leonardo used the same smile in a number of his paintings.

Much has also been made about the *Mona Lisa's* 'uncommonly thick' eyebrows, a belief which came about after Vasari wrote a description of the painting. A close examination of the above detail shows there aren't any eyebrows; women of the time commonly shaved these off. Vasari had never seen the Mona Lisa and though it is popular to quote his text on the painting it must be realised he wrote his treatise based entirely upon hearsay. Despite this, he was totally accurate in stating that, "On looking at the pit of the throat one could swear that the pulses were beating."

The most expressive parts of the human face are the outer points of the lips and eyes. Leonardo has deliberately left these areas in shadow which creates the effect of causing different people to read different emotions on the face of the sitter, whomever she may be.

Mona Lisa is distinguished by her complete absence of jewellery whereas the norm for the day was to present subjects with elaborate decoration as can be seen in the painting done by Titan of Caterina Cornaro, Queen Of Cyprus. Mona Lisa's hair is smooth with only the covering of a black veil, hands are free of rings or bracelets and nothing adorns her neck. There are small intricate loops across the neckline of her dress; such was Leonardo's interest in codes that many people have searched in vain for a message in these loops. This painting went against all the trends of the time and is a perfect example of how Leonardo never followed traditions. He abandoned the usual poses, which had subjects shown as stiff and upright, replacing this with a relaxed sitter, her beautifully painted hands resting easily on the arm of her chair.

While most people are aware the *Mona Lisa* is also called *La Gioconda* by the Italians (translation: "a light-hearted woman."), fewer know the French refer to it as *La Joconde.* Done in oils on poplar wood it was originally much larger than it is today. Two columns on either side of *Mona Lisa h*ave been cut off making it difficult to recognize she was seated on a terrace. The bases of these columns can just be seen on the very edges of the painting which now measures only 77 x 53 cms.

At the time Leonardo painted the *Mona Lisa* he was also doing some of his finest sketches of plant life and nature. This can be clearly seen in the background of the panel and it is very elaborate, perhaps the finest he ever did. The bridge shown has now been identified as being at Buriano (Arezzo).

The painting of *Mona Lisa* has had an interesting history being stolen on the 21st August 1911 from an Italian thief who had taken the painting to Italy. The loss of the painting was not reported for twenty-four hours as most employees assumed it had been removed by the official museum photographer. It then took a week to search the 49-acre Louvre with the only find being the painting's frame, which was located in a staircase. It resurfaced some two years later in Florence, when an Italian named Vincenzo Perugia offered to sell the painting to the Uffizi Gallery for US$100,000. It was exhibited for a time and then returned to Paris.

To steal the painting Perugia had spent a night hiding in a little-used room at the Louvre. While the museum was closed he simply walked into the room where the *Mona*

Lisa was hung, removed it from the wall then cut it from the frame once he reached the staircase. He then exited the building breaking out through a 'locked' door by unscrewing the doorknob. Ten months prior to the theft the Louvre had made the decision to begin having their masterpieces placed under glass. Perugia was one of four men assigned to the job and so in a position to get to know the Louvre well enough to pull off the crime.

In 1956 acid was thrown on the lower half of the painting with the required restoration taking some years.

The situation today is that the *Mona Lisa* has become so well-known that it may only be viewed behind thick protective glass after battling through a large crowd of sightseers. The cover of triplex glass which protects the painting was gifted by the Japanese during the *Mona Lisa's* 1974 visit to Japan -- that being the last time it left the museum. By international agreement the painting will no longer be displayed in other countries but will stay safely on display at the Louvre in Paris where it may be properly protected against further damage, theft or attack. The bulletproof box is kept at a constant 68 degrees Fahrenheit with a humidity of 55 percent; a built-in air conditioner and nine pounds of silica gel ensure no change in the air condition. Once a year the box is opened to check the painting and for maintenance on the air conditioning system.

Time may have cracked and crazed the paintwork of the *Mona Lisa,* but the air of mystery remains. It has been endlessly reproduced, has inspired numerous writers, poets and musicians, yet remains little understood. The same style can be seen used by other masters such as Raphael (*Maddalena Doni*) and Carot (*Dame à la Perle*). Many naked women have been painted or drawn in the attitude of the *Mona Lisa* and these were a favorite on the occasions when artists were called on to portray royals in their baths. The Carrara Academy in Bergamo has just one of many nude versions, this one having been painted in the 17th century. Copying of the *Mona Lisa* style started even before the painting was finished.

By far the most controversial version of the Mona Lisa is in the Vernon collection in the U.S. This painting clearly shows the columns on either side of the sitter which have been cut off the Louvre example. The owners consider the artwork to be authentic and value it at $2.5 million.

The last work done on the panel was in the 1950's when age spots were removed during a cleaning. Suggestions that the painting should experience a thorough facelift involving the removal of layers of resin, lacquer and varnish from the past 500 years have received a firm thumbs down from the Louvre. Computer restoration shows that the colors of the painting may be quite different without the grime that presently covers it. Rosy cheeks instead of sickly yellow, pale blue skies instead of the present green glow. On the downside, any attempt to clean the painting may result in irreparable damage from the various solvents required to remove the varnish and there is no guarantee the suspected bright colors exist below the coatings which have been applied over the years as a protectant. For those lucky enough to have viewed the work under natural light state there is still a surprising amount of color evident to the eye, maybe more is below the grime, but no one dares to clean her. X-rays have shown there are three different versions of the *Mona Lisa* hidden under the present one.

SECRETS AND THEORIES

Speculations about Mona Lisa

Columns and Trimming:

Scientists and historians have been arguing for a long time that after Leonardo's death the painting was cut down by having part of the panel at both sides removed. Early depicts of Mona Lisa depict columns on both sides of the figure. However, in the original painting, only the edges of the bases can be seen.

Some art historians, such as Martin Kemp, now argue that the painting has not been altered, the columns depicted in the copies were added by the copyists. This view was bolstered during 2004 and 2005 when 39 international team of specialists undertook the most through scientific examination of the Mona Lisa ever. A "reserve" was discovered around all four edges of the panel, beneath the frame. A reserve is an area of bare wood surrounding the gessoed and painted portion of the panel. The team revealed that this is in fact a genuine reserve, not a result of removal of the gesso or paint like most thought. A raised edge of the reserve still existing around the gesso, the result of build up from the edge of brush strokes at the edge of the gesso area proves that.

We know that, to fit a frame, the reserve area have been trimmed at some point. However, at no point has any of Leonardo's actual paint been trimmed. So we come to the conclusion that the columns in early copies must be inventions of those artists, or copies of another studio version of Mona Lisa.

Copies

It has been suggested that Leonardo painted more than one version of the Mona Lisa. One of the strongest contender is the "Isleworth Mona Lisa", which had been hidden in a Swiss bank vault for forty years before being unveiled to the public on September 27, 2012. The Swiss Federal Institute of Technology in Zurich has dated the piece to Leonardo's lifetime, and an expert in sacred geometry says it conforms to the artist's basic line structures.

People also made the same claim about the version in the Vernon collection. This is especially interesting because it was originally part of the collection at the Louvre. Another version was given to Joshua Reynolds by the Duke of Leeds in exchange for a Reynolds self-portrait. Reynolds claimed that his was the original one and the French one was the copy, which had been disproved of course. It is however, a good point that it was copied when the original's colors were far brighter than they are now. The painting is in a private collection now, but exhibited at the Dulwich Picture Gallery in 2006.

Museo del Prado in Madrid announced that it had discovered and almost fully restored a copy of the painting by a pupil of Leonardo, very possibly alongside the master, in January 2012. We can guess what the original portrait looked like at the time from the copy, since the varnish on the original has become cracked and yellowed with age.

German imaging researchers performed further analysis of the Museo del Prado version, comparing it to Da Vinci's Mona Lisa, and in May 2014 speculated that, based on perspective analysis of key features in the images, the two images were painted at the same time from slightly different viewpoints. They further proposed that two images may therefore form a stereoscopic pair, creating the illusion of 3-dimensional depth, when viewed side by side.

Nude versions

Mona Lisa appears nude in several copies of the original painting, suggesting that they were copied from a lost Leonardo original depicting Lisa naked. Most famous of them is the painting done by Salai, Nude Woman (Donna Nuda) and Mona Vanna.

Infrared scan

In 2004, experts from the National Research Council of Canada conducted a three-dimensional infrared scan. Because of the aging of the varnish on the painting it is difficult to discern details. Data from the scan and infrared were used by Bruno Mottin of the French Museums' "Center for Research and Restoration" to argue that the transparent gauze veil worn by the sitter is a guarnello, typically used by women while pregnant or just after giving birth. A similar guarnello was painted by Sandro Botticelli in his *Portrait of Smeralda Brandini*, depicting a pregnant woman on display in the Victoria and Albert Museum in London. Furthermore, this reflectography revealed that *Mona Lisa*'s hair is not loosely hanging down, but seems attached at the back of the head to a bonnet or pinned back into a chignon and covered with a veil, bordered with a sombre rolled hem. In the 16th century, hair hanging loosely down on the shoulders was the customary style of unmarried young women or prostitutes. This apparent contradiction with her status as a married woman has now been resolved.

Researchers also used the data to reveal details about the technique used and to predict that the painting will degrade very little if current conservation techniques are continued. During 2006, *Mona Lisa* underwent a major scientific observation that proved through infrared cameras she was originally wearing a bonnet and clutching her chair, something that da Vinci decided to change as an afterthought.

Eyebrows and eyelashes

Why Mona Lisa has only very faint eyebrows and apparently no eyelashes? This has always been a long lasting mystery of the painting. However, in October 2007, a French engineer and inventor Pascal Cotte stated that he had discovered with a high-definition camera that Leonardo originally did paint eyebrows and eyelashes.

By an ultra-high resolution close-up that magnified Mona Lisa's face 24 times, Cotte says he found a single brushstroke of a single hair above the left eye. The engineer states that other eyebrow hairs that potentially could have appeared on the painting may have faded or been inadvertently erased by a poor attempt to clean the painting. The Cotte's works also uncovered the proof that her hands were originally painted in a slightly different position than in the final portrait, according to the engineer.

Vasari also describes the painting as having thick eyebrows. This could mean two things: either the eyebrows and lashes were accidently removed or Vasari didn't see the painting himself.

Subject

Although once the sitter has identified as Lisa del Giocondo, a lack of evidence has long fueled alternative theories. IN the last year of his life, da Vinci spoke of a portrait "of a certain Florentine lady done from life at the request of the magnificent Giuliano de' Medici." There is no evidence found that could create a link between Lisa del Giocondo and Giuliano de' Medici. However the comment could refer to one of the two other portraits of women executed by Leonardo.

Lillian Schwartz of Bell Labs suggests that the Mona Lisa is actually a self-portrait. She created this theory with the results of a digital analysis of the facial features of the woman in the painting and those of the famous Portrait of a Man in Red Chalk.

Sigmund Freud stated that the half-smile was a recovered memory of Leonardo's mother. Some people also suggest that there was no model, Leonardo was painting an ideal woman.

Some people believes that the sitter is Isabelle of Aragon, the Duchess of Milan. Leonardo was the court painter for the Duke of Milan for almost eleven years. The pattern on

Mona Lisa's dark green dress may indicate that she was a member of the house of Sforza.

Historian Giuseppe Pallanti published Mona Lisa Revealed: The True Identity of Leonardo's Model in 2004. According to the author, Leonardo's father was a friend of del Giocondo:"The portrait of *Mona Lisa*, done when Lisa del Giocondo was aged about 24, was probably commissioned by Leonardo's father himself for his friends as he is known to have done on at least one other occasion." he says. In 2007, genealogist Domenico Savini identified the princesses Natalia and Irina Strozzi as descendants of Lisa del Giocondo. Scan data obtained in 2004 suggested that the painting dated from around 1503 and commemorated the birth of the Giocondo's second son. The sitter in the painting was also pregnant according to some sources.

Art historian Silvano Vincenti claimed Leonardo's lover and apprentice Salai was the inspiration and figure for the painting. In December 2010 Italian art historian Silvano Vinceti reported that the Mona Lisa appears to have tiny letters and numbers in her eyes which are only apparent when viewed with a magnifying glass and shortly afterwards said that the model was Leonardo's male apprentice Gian Giacomo Caprotti (known as Salai) and that the letters were clues to his identity. The Louvre, pointing out that he had had no access to the actual painting, said that after "every laboratory test possible" in 2004 and 2009 that "no inscriptions, letters or numbers, were discovered during the tests." and that "The ageing of the painting on wood has caused a great number of cracks to appear in the paint, which have caused a number of shapes to appear that have often been subject to over-interpretation".

Pregnancy

The clue is something she wore when she sit for the painting. Researchers studying 3D images of the Mona Lisa states that she was probably either pregnant or had just given birth.

Scans revealed an evidence of a fine veil around Mona Lisa's shoulders. Which would mean that she was expecting during the Italian Renaissance.

The veil darkened as the painting aged. The thick and dark varnish on the work didn't make it easier to know what color her dress really is either. The piece of fabric draped over her shoulder was sometimes interpreted as a shawl or a scarf.

However, images obtained from infrared reflectography shows us that the veil also called a guarnello is actually transparent. The scans also reveal that Mona Lisa doesn't have her hair down as it appears. A large part of her tresses are pinned back into a chignon and covered with a veil.

The "S" and "L"

Silvanto Vinceti, who also claimed that the Mona Lisa in fact is Salai himself, claims he has found the letter "S" in the model's left eye, the letter "L" in her right eye, and the number "72" under the arched bridge in the backdrop of Leonardo da Vinci's famous painting.

The symbols Vinceti found are not visible to the naked eye. Vincenti said that they are " very small, painted with a tiny brush and subjected to the tear and wear of time."

However, he didn't study the painting directly at the Louvre Museum, as the officers of the Louvre Museum stated. . He said his research was based on high-definition scanned images from the Lumiere Technology in Paris, which specializes in digitizing artworks.

Golden triangle, rectangle and spiral

As can be seen in this picture of the Mona Lisa, Da Vinci appears to have used the Golden Rectangle to bring balance and depth into the painting. The Golden Rectangle was believed by artists to be the most aesthetically pleasing quadrangle. In addition to the Golden Rectangle, Da Vinci, a mathematician as well as an artist, used the Golden Triangle to draw attention to the

Mona Lisa's face. The Mona Lisa's body from elbow to elbow to the top of the head forms the Golden Triangle. A triangle, by virtue of its shape, naturally draws the eye up.

Da Vinci further incorporated math in art by first placing a Golden Rectangle just above the Mona Lisa's nose. By adding squares to the first rectangle using Fibonacci's series, Da Vinci formed what is termed the Golden Spiral.

The large Golden Rectangle is thus formed. The base of the rectangle is formed by a line that extends from the wrist to the elbow. Its sides are formed by extending a line up to the top of the head.

While the Golden Rectangle is thought to be aesthetically pleasing, the Golden Spiral is thought to draw the person into a painting. Spirals naturally cause the eye to pull to the center.

The Last Supper

Food

Why did da Vinci picked those particular foods? The foods he chose don't correspond to what Evangelists described. Although some far-fetched hypotheses in the Da Vinci Code are wrong, we can agree that Leonardo included symbols and commentary in his depiction. He attempted to confuse and fool the observer with contradictory symbols and double-meanings.

In the painting, a salt shaker tipped over in front of Judas. A fallen saltshaker is traditionally a sign of bad luck. Once can say that it indicates the mischief of Judas. The fallen saltshaker could suggest his rehabilitation.

Judas is also the only one with an empty plate in front of him. It could mean that he is full and mischievous or that he is the only one who isn't fooled.

The fish on the table is clearly a reminder that Jesus spent most of his life around Lake Tiberias and that he selected his Apostles among local fishermen. However, it isn't clear whether the fish is herring or eel. Some people argue that da Vinci was deliberately ambiguous about the species of fish. Eel in Italian is aringa, although when it is spelled arringa it means indoctrination. And herring in northern Italy is renga, meaning he who denies religion.

Mary Magdalene

According to some historians, Mary Magdalane, rather than apostle John, sits on Jesus' right in the painting.

Mirrored Version

Slavisa Pesci, an information technologist, created an interesting visual effect by overlaying a semitransparent, mirrored version of the painting on top of the original. The final result is very interesting to say at least.

Two figures that look like Templar knights appear at both ends of the table, while someone possibly holding an infant stands to Jesus' left. There is also the presence of a previously unseen wine goblet in front of Jesus. According to Pesci, it may be a depiction of the first Eucharist, when Jesus gave his disciples bread and wine at the Last Supper to represent his body and blood. It isn't indicated that who the child could be, but some scholars have said it's the child of Jesus and Mary Magdalene.

The Knife

Some people previously stated that a disembodied hand was holding the knife present in the painting. The knife is almost certainly a dinner knife, not a weapon. Also, analysis of the painting shows that Peter holds the knife, though he does so in an odd position.

The Music

Musicians have speculated that the true hidden message in *The Last Supper* is actually an accompanying soundtrack. In 2007, Italian musician Giovanni Maria Pala created 40 seconds of a somber song using notes supposedly encoded within da Vinci's distinctive composition.

ENDING

I am writing these books mostly for people to recognize the great talent of the great masters and spread them. I hope you got what you came for. I would love to hear your view on my book. Please leave an honest review on my Amazon page and don't forget to check out my other books too. Have a good life!

Other Works Recommended For You

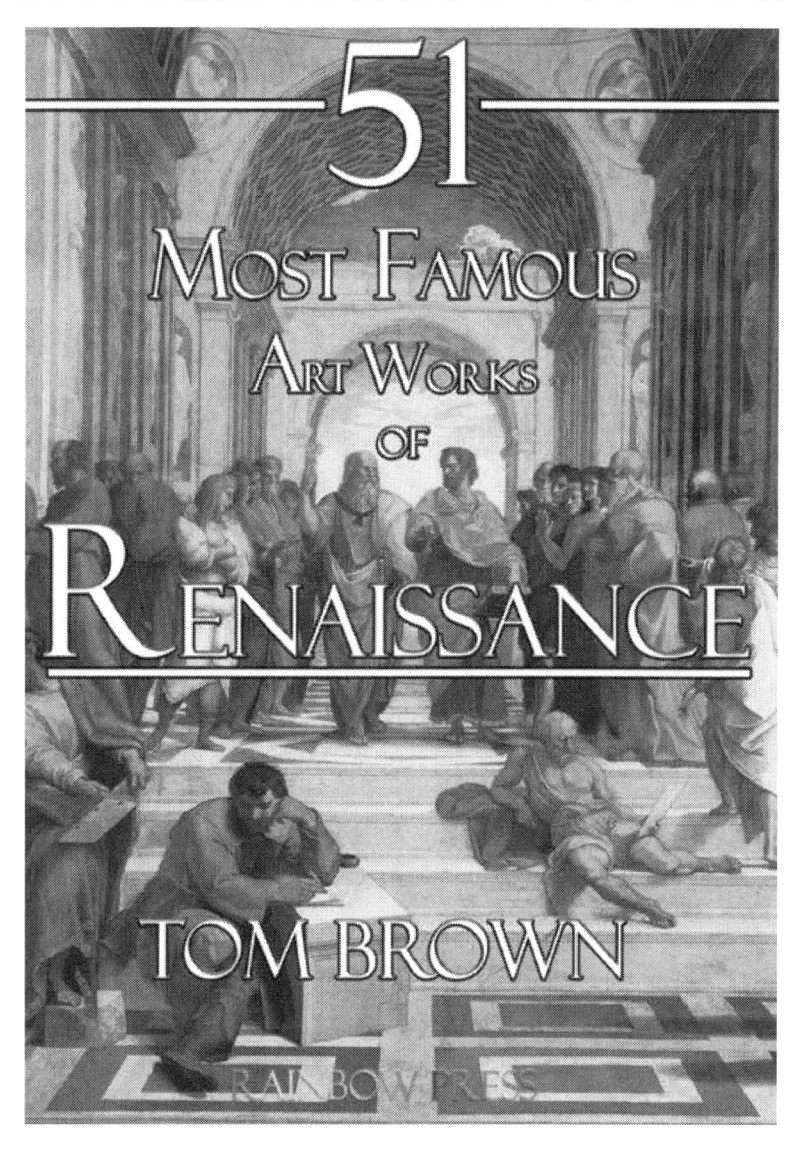

51 MOST FAMOUS ART WORKS OF RENAISSANCE

TOM BROWN

51 Most Famous Art Works of Renaissance:

Analysis and Description of Art Works From da Vinci, Michelangelo, Raphael, Titian and More...

51 Most Famous Art Works of Renaissance:

Analysis and Description of Art Works From da Vinci, Michelangelo, Raphael, Titian and More...

Leonardo da Vinci

Michelangelo di Lodovico Buonarroti Simoni

Donato di Niccolò di Betto Bardi (Donatello)

Raffaello Sanzio da Urbino (Raphael)

Michelangelo Merisi da Caravaggio

Tiziano Vecellio (Titian)

Andrea del Verrocchio

Paolo Veronese

Giorgione

All the great artists from Renaissance came together and created masterpieces. Little did they know that their works would still create awe in the hearts of those who gaze upon them for the centuries to come.

Renaissance is an era in which mankind **advanced** in every possible aspect. But most important of them, in my opinion, was **ART**.

Some of them were lucky, some of them weren't; but one thing is certain:

They were all GREAT ARTISTS!!

Read and find out why and how these artists created the most wonderful masterpieces of history!!

In this book you are going to find:

- *Analysis of Paintings and Statues*
- *Interesting Stories Regarding Those Masterpieces*
- *Interesting Facts About the Masters and Their Works*
- *Stories From History*
- *Method of the Greatest Artists*
- *Secrets, Theories and Surprises.*

You Are Also Going To Find Out:

❖ *How Did Michelangelo Paint a Ceiling?*

- *Where Did Leonardo Learn How to Paint The Last Supper on a Wall?*

- *How Did Leonardo Choose Models for The Last Supper?*

- *Who Was The Mysterious Subject of Mona Lisa?*

- *Why Does Mona Lisa Smile and Stare at the Same Time?*

- *Who Influenced Raphael?*

- *How Did Veronese Paint His "The Wedding at Cana"; a Painting Which Measures 67.29 m^2 ?*

- *How Did French Soldiers Carry "The Wedding at Cana" Across the Country?*

- *Which Symbols Did Leonardo da Vinci Hide in His Paintings?*

Read Now And:

- *Learn Great Things About the Hidden History of Renaissance Art*
- *Learn How to Describe and Analyze Paintings and Statues*
- *Learn How Did Masters From Renaissance Think*

Buy This Book Now

AND

Enjoy Knowing More Than Others

Michelangelo: Biography, Stories and Anecdotes. Interesting Stories, Thrilling Adventures and Curious Events

We all know Leonardo da Vinci was the greatest artist of Renaissance. He went beyond what is expected. But surely there are some artists, whom can be a rival for da Vinci. Take a look at what they had accomplished and choose for yourself. Who is the "Renaissance Man"?

I have published THE right book for you. The stories of Michelangelo.

Michelangelo was an artists who were deeply in love with statues. He loved carving, shaping and DESTROYING them. Yes, he liked to destroy his own works. But his work on Sistine Chapel, David, Moses proves he knew something. One of the greatest artist of all time, better than da Vinci according to some, Michelangelo knew how to make his life colorful.

Grab my book now for only 0.99$ and witness it with your own eyes, as if you were living it.

[Michelangelo: Biography, Stories and Anecdotes. Interesting Stories, Thrilling Adventures and Curious Events](#)